Recovering Sarepta, A Phoenician City

Recovering Sarepta, A Phoenician City

EXCAVATIONS AT SARAFAND, LEBANON, 1969-1974, BY THE UNIVERSITY MUSEUM
OF THE UNIVERSITY OF PENNSYLVANIA

JAMES B. PRITCHARD

PRINCETON UNIVERSITY PRESS, PRINCETON, NEW JERSEY

1978

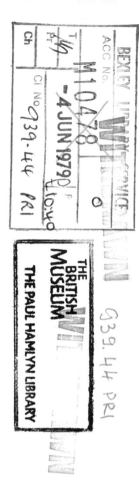
COPYRIGHT © 1978 BY PRINCETON UNIVERSITY PRESS

PUBLISHED BY PRINCETON UNIVERSITY PRESS, PRINCETON, NEW JERSEY

IN THE UNITED KINGDOM: PRINCETON UNIVERSITY PRESS, GUILDFORD, SURREY

LIBRARY OF CONGRESS CATALOGING IN PUBLICATION DATA WILL
BE FOUND ON THE LAST PRINTED PAGE OF THIS BOOK

THIS BOOK HAS BEEN COMPOSED IN LINOTYPE ELECTRA

DESIGNED BY BRUCE CAMPBELL

PRINTED IN THE UNITED STATES OF AMERICA
BY PRINCETON UNIVERSITY PRESS, PRINCETON, NEW JERSEY

TITLE PAGE: "SIGN OF TANIT" DRAWN FROM FIGURE 104.

Contents

List of Illustrations

LIST OF ILLUSTRATIONS

Preface

A well-informed Egyptian scribe who lived about 1200 B.C. would have known something of Phoenician geography—the names of Byblos, Beirut, Sidon, Sarepta, Tyre, for example. So, at least, it would seem from a satirical letter written on papyrus by an Egyptian official, whose name was Hori.[1]

Hori addressed some good-natured raillery to a scribal opponent whom he considered incompetent. By reciting what was patently obvious to an educated scribe and demanding an answer, the Egyptian official displayed the general ignorance of his correspondent. "Let me tell thee," he wrote sardonically, "of another strange city, named Byblos. What is it like? And its goddess? . . . Pray, instruct me about Beirut, about Sidon and Sarepta. . . . They say, another town is in the sea, named Tyre-the-Port. . . ."

The report on our excavations at Sarepta presented in the following pages could be considered a belated response to the taunt of Hori: "Pray, instruct me about . . . Sarepta." A famous city in the thirteenth century B.C., it was soon to be eclipsed by Tyre and Sidon, both of which became more prosperous and prominent. Yet an occasional mention of the city in Assyrian inscriptions, the Bible, and Greek and Latin writings testifies to its survival. Beyond these scattered and sometimes cryptic references to Sarepta—valuable as they are as a general historical framework—little remains in the written record to instruct us in detail.

The record within the ruins at Sarepta has proved to be more instructive. In five working seasons since 1969, we have cut down through the accumulation of debris from more than two thousand years of the city's history, reaching finally the bedrock on which the first settlement was founded about 1600 B.C. We have cleared the sand from the quay from which Roman and Byzantine ships sailed for other Mediterranean ports; discovered streets, houses, pots, and tools; and found potters' kilns and workshops used in the very century in which the Egyptian official made his satirical remark involving Sarepta. The names of some of the people who lived there have been found incised on pottery and ivory; even the name of the city itself has appeared neatly carved in stone on a stamp seal. Mentioned also are the gods who were revered, and

---

[1] Translated by J. A. Wilson in James B. Pritchard, ed., *Ancient Near Eastern Texts Relating to the Old Testament*, 3rd ed., 1969, (hereafter: *ANET*[3]), pp. 475-79.

a small shrine built beside the industrial area of the city has borne witness to the kinds of offerings which were made to two goddesses of fertility.

These and other discoveries serve to document the history of a particular city. Yet, what has been found at Sarepta has a significance for the cultural history of one of the important peoples of the ancient world. The Phoenicians, whose exploits and achievements have been widely acclaimed by their neighbors, have been poorly served by archaeology. There have been chance discoveries in their homeland and archaeological evidence from their colonies, but until the discovery of the Phoenician levels at Sarepta there had been no excavation of a stratified urban site on the coast of Lebanon that had been inhabited over the centuries when the famous seafarers had planted their colonies in the West. That our findings at Sarepta may be seen in the perspective of what has been known about Phoenician culture we have described in Chapter II the extant sources for the Phoenicians before presenting in detail the results of our excavations.

Our work at Sarepta has extended over a period of eight years. The site was chosen in the summer of 1968, after an extensive survey of Lebanese sites that appeared to have remains from the Iron Age. Excavation began with an eight-week campaign in June and July of 1969. For each of the next three years excavation was continued

at the site for ten-week periods during the months of April, May, and June. During the spring season of 1973, when serious disturbances in Lebanon precluded any field work, six members of the staff worked with artifacts stored in the National Museum in Beirut to prepare the material for the publication of a preliminary report. A fifth season of excavation took place in the spring of 1974, but in 1975 fighting in Lebanon made it impossible to work, except for some further study of artifacts from the previous seasons which had been stored in Beirut. All told, 50 weeks have been expended in full-scale excavations at the site; but the additional labor which has been devoted to the project by members of the staff in drawing, photographing, research, and writing cannot be so easily computed.

For the first season a staff of seven proved adequate. John E. Huesman, who taught at Alma College in California and had worked on a half dozen expeditions in Jordan, agreed to take over the administrative duties. He drove the Land Rover, took care of payroll and purchased equipment when he was not serving as an area supervisor. Thomas L. McClellan, with four years of experience in the excavations at Tell es-Sa'idiyeh, Jordan, finished the classes which he taught at Bowie State College in Maryland and joined us. Two graduate students at the American University of Beirut, Martha Joukowsky and Leila

Badre, readily agreed to join the staff, as did Leila Khalidy from the same institution. Pierre Bikai, from the Tyre excavations, assumed the responsibility for surveying and drawing the plans. Finally, Magnus Ottosson came from Sweden as soon as he finished his Ph.D. at Uppsala. Thus, with a Swede, a Syrian—Leila Badre came from Latakia—two Lebanese, and four Americans, we assembled a congenial and knowledgeable staff for the first season.

In subsequent seasons we were joined by others. The largest contingent consisted of graduate students in archaeology: from the University of Pennsylvania there were William P. Anderson, Ellen Herscher, Issam Khalifeh, and Patrick McGovern; Homer Athanassiou came from the University of Missouri; Patricia Cecil Bikai, from the Graduate Theological Union in Berkeley; Julia Costello had been studying American archaeology at the University of Colorado; Giocchino Falsone, a native of Sicily, was working on a degree at the University of Chicago; Holly Hartquist was doing a dissertation at the Sorbonne; Adrianna Hopper and Susan Long were graduate students at the American University of Beirut; Marian Laaff came from Harvard, where she was working on ceramic technology; Sigurdur Orm Steingrimsson, an Icelander, was writing his dissertation at Uppsala. In addition to these students there were Pierre Proulx, who had had his doctorate from Johns Hopkins and was teaching at the Pontifical

Biblical Institute in Rome; and William Stiebing, who after gaining his Ph.D. at the University of Pennsylvania, was teaching at the University of Louisiana in New Orleans. To this group of 22 much of the credit belongs for the success we had through the five seasons.

Labor was readily available from the village of Sarafand. The size of the labor force varied: usually 50 men were hired at the beginning of a season; as the work progressed the number was increased gradually, reaching at times as many as 125. In time it was discovered that laborers could be trained to perform tasks which were normally done by the staff, such as restoring pots, counting and marking sherds with India ink, and even drawing profiles of pots and other objects. Thus freed from these routine jobs, staff members were able to accept more important responsibilities.

In addition to staff and laborers others have made important contributions. Julian and Eunice Whittlesey and Bruce Bevan took aerial photographs of the site from a hydrogen balloon; other photography was done by National Geographic Magazine photographers Otis Imboden and Robert Azzi; Jack R. Sims, Jr., and Peter T. Sturken mapped the southern harbor, diving with scuba equipment; Elizabeth Ralph analyzed the Carbon-14 samples in the laboratory of the Museum Applied Science Center for Archaeology; Frederick Matson interpreted certain features of the kilns; drawings were done by various members of the staff and Rune Ødegaarden, Helga Seeden, Yolande Steger, Elizabeth Simpson, and Jane Homiller; pots were reconstructed by Yvette Bridi and Mouna Basile Sehnaoui; the hoard of Byzantine coins was catalogued and studied by Marcus Arguelles; skeletal remains from the burials were studied by Larry S. Kobori; Gloria Dale provided a classification of the glass; David I. Owen contributed a study of the Ugaritic inscription; and Javier Teixidor interpreted the Phoenician inscriptions.

Financial support of the excavations—transportation and board for the staff (no salaries were paid), labor, equipment, rental of the land, photographic supplies, shipping, and insurance—has been generously supplied by an anonymous foundation, the Committee on Research and Exploration of the National Geographic Society, the University Museum of the University of Pennsylvania, and the Ford Foundation, which provided support for graduate students through its trainee program. William Chandler, President of the Trans-Arabian Pipe-Line Company, made available within the Sidon Terminal at Zahrani a large dormitory that served as living quarters for the staff during five seasons. The American University of Beirut allowed the use of rooms where artifacts could be stored and studied.

Finally the hospitality and assistance of the host country of Lebanon must be acknowledged. Not only did Emir Maurice Chehab, Director General of the Service des Antiquités, obtain from the President of the Republic of Lebanon a decree which gave the University of Pennsylvania a concession for archaeological work at Sarafand for a period of six years but he provided help in solving the many problems that arose throughout each of the seasons. In addition, two other members of the Service, M. Roger Saidah and M. Brahim Kawkabani, rendered valuable services to the project.

Apart from the news releases written at the end of each campaign, this volume is the first general report of our excavations intended for the non-specialist reader. A technical preliminary report on the Roman port was published in the *Bulletin du Musée de Beyrouth*, vol. 24, 1971, pp. 39–56; and my monograph (with contributions by William P. Anderson, Ellen Herscher, and Javier Teixidor), *Sarepta: A Preliminary Report on the Iron Age*, was published in 1975 as a University Museum Monograph. Those concerned with more detailed descriptions, drawings, and references for some of the materials in this book, may find them in these two reports, which are addressed primarily to archaeologists.

April 6, 1977, University Museum
University of Pennsylvania

J.B.P.

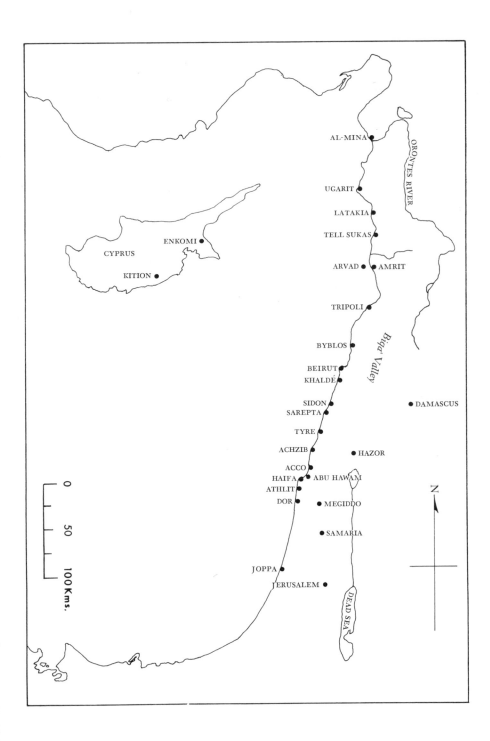

AL-MINA

ORONTES RIVER

UGARIT

LATAKIA

TELL SUKAS

ENKOMI

CYPRUS

ARVAD ● AMRIT

KITION

TRIPOLI

BYBLOS

Biqa' Valley

BEIRUT
KHALDÉ

SIDON
SAREPTA

DAMASCUS

TYRE

ACHZIB

HAZOR

ACCO
HAIFA ● ABU HAWAM
ATHLIT
DOR

N

MEGIDDO

SAMARIA

0

50

JOPPA

JERUSALEM

100 Kms.

DEAD SEA

1. Photograph of the Phoenician coast from Beirut to Mt. Carmel, taken on June 30, 1973, by the Earth Resources Technology Satellite from a height of 914 km.

I

Sarafand: The Site of Sarepta

THE strip of the Lebanese coast which Sarepta had once occupied was viewed in a new perspective on the morning of June 30, 1973. At precisely 9:33 A.M. that Saturday, an area of the earth's surface known today as Sarafand in Lebanon came within view of the three cameras of the Earth Resources Technology Satellite, which had been launched 342 days before from Vandenberg Air Force Base in California.[1] The satellite was traveling southward at a height of 914 km. above the earth—a distance as great as that from Sarafand to Baghdad. Within 30 seconds the satellite's sensors had scanned an area 185 km. square and transmitted to earth a clear picture of Sarepta and its neighbors (Fig. 1).

Eighty km. to the south, at the head of a mountain range, is Mt. Carmel, where the legendary prophet Elijah had engaged in contest with the prophets of the Phoenician Baal. Tyre is seen only 22 km. distant, at the tip of a promontory that had once been the island from which a colonists had sailed to found new cities in Africa and Europe. To the north, Sidon is distinguishable, a mere 13 km. up the coast; and beyond is Beirut, a Phoenician port which has grown in modern times into a major center of world trade. Across the Lebanon ranges, Damascus, inhabited continuously since Phoenician days, appears in the picture as a dark spot of vegetation within the great Syrian desert. Such was the historical geography caught by the lens of an electronic miracle, the moth-shaped ERTS vehicle that flew silently and unobserved by the villagers of Sarafand as they went about their work on a morning in June.

There are some 1,500 Shiite Moslems—the 1965 census lists a resident population of 1,459—in Sarafand today. A few eke out a living from fishing; but most are engaged in growing lemons, oranges, and bananas in the irrigated land that flanks the coast. Although the modern Sarafandi dresses in European clothes and makes use of western technology, his life style is rooted in the traditional culture of the Middle East, reaching as far back as the time of the biblical patriarchs and Hammurabi; hospitality, a sense of personal dignity, reliance on the spoken word

[1] Thomas H. Maugh II, "ERTS: Surveying Earth's Resources from Space," *Science*, 180, no. 4081, 1973, pp. 49-51; *idem*, "ERTS (II): A New Way of Viewing the Earth," *Science*, 180, no. 4082, 1973, pp. 171-73.

2. Air view of the two promontories at Sarafand, Ras el-Qantara at top center and Ras esh-Shiq at lower left; and adjacent excavations as they appeared at the end of the 1970 season

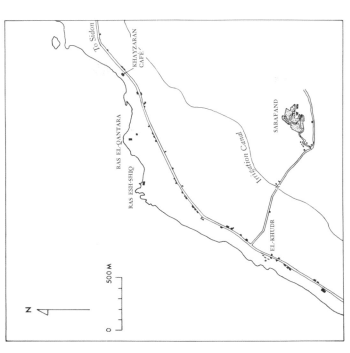

N

0   500 M

3. Map of Sarafand and vicinity

as binding, and a persistent instinct for courtesy which shows in a hyperbole of speech and graceful gestures—such ancient values have survived and are readily apparent under a western facade.

Yet it was within an inconspicuous *tell* beside the sea at Sarafand that the more tangible remnants of the past were to become evident. After an hour's drive from Beirut, 50 km. to the north, one reaches the village of Sarafand at the Khayzaran Cafe (Figs. 2 and 3). Just beyond, a dirt road to the west leads to a low mound on a promontory, called Ras el-Qantara, jutting out 100 m. into the sea. From this now deserted *tell* one can see the white stone houses of the modern village of Sarafand in the hills to the south.

The timing of our first visit in July 1968 was propitious. During the recent winter's storms heavy seas had cut into the side of the mound and displayed its contents (Fig. 4). It was not a natural formation of stone and soil but the accumulation of ancient human occupation. A clear plan of a house could be traced, with only the wall next to the sea missing; and strewn over the sand were blocks of masonry and a well-turned column made of marble brought from a distant quarry (Fig. 5). Potsherds could be picked up by the hundreds.

From the handles of amphorae, rims of delicate bowls, bits of ribbed ware from the walls of storage vessels, terra

5. Marble column and building blocks on the beach at Ras el-Qantara

4. Walls of Roman building at Ras el-Qantara which were uncovered by the sea during a storm of 1968

sigillata—scores of diagnostic sherds—it was easy to see that the ruins unearthed by the winter's storm belonged to the first few centuries of the Christian era. How much earlier men had built and lived there was not learned for another two years—and then only after a wide search and the removal of tons of debris.

Farmers, too, had uncovered antiquities. Scattered about the cultivated fields on top of the mound were sections of large columns, which because of their size could only have come from a public building, other worked architectural elements and an occasional mill from an olive press—ancient artifacts which farmers had found too large to move or break with a sledge hammer. It was obvious that some valuable evidence for the archaeological history of the site had already been lost and more was endangered by deep plowing as well as by erosion from the sea.

It was difficult to estimate precisely the area of the ancient settlement. The mound was discernible only along its northern and western sides, where it rises sharply to a height of about 12 m. above the level of the sea (Fig. 6). In terracing their fields for irrigation, landowners had erased any indications that may have existed of the southern and eastern limits of urban occupation.

Some 500 m. southwest of the promontory of Ras el-Qantara there is a second projection, called Ras esh-Shiq,

beside which is a moon-shaped bay that could easily have provided a safe anchorage for ships. Potsherds could be seen throughout this area and even for another half kilometer of the coast to the south of Ras esh-Shiq. Apparently the city, in the Roman period at least, had extended for a kilometer along the coast.

In addition to the surface evidence there was another clue to the site's antiquity. Sarafand, spelled as it is in Arabic today with the consonants *ṣrfnd*, has long been recognized as similar to the ancient Sarepta, *ṣrpt*. In fact, the modern spelling could easily be a corruption of the older. In both names the first two letters are identical; the change from *p* to *f* is normal; and it is quite possible that the more ancient *t* had become the *nd* at the end of Sarafand. Place names are notoriously long-lived, often surviving conquests, destructions, and even a change in the language spoken by the indigenous population. For example, one writes Tyre in Arabic with the same consonants that a scribe would have used as he chiseled the name of the city in Phoenician letters on a stone stela three thousand years ago. Only the script has changed. If, then, the equation of Sarafand with Sarepta is correct, the importance of the ruins beside the sea would be further enhanced by the written sources which mention Sarepta as a Phoenician and Roman city.

The brief visit to Sarafand on July 31, 1968, was but

one of more than a score of excursions we made that summer to sites of antiquity in Lebanon. Emir Maurice Chehab, Director General of the Service des Antiquités of Lebanon, had responded favorably to a proposal of the University Museum of the University of Pennsylvania to begin a long-range archaeological project in Lebanon and had suggested several possible sites.

The law governing the disposal of antiquities in Lebanon is generous to the excavator in that it provides him with a share of the movable ones for display in the museum of the sponsoring institution.[2] Obviously, objects of major importance for the history of the country are to be reserved for the National Museum in Beirut. But what remains is to be divided equally. The law, written in 1933, when France exercised a protectorate over the Lebanon, offers a simple solution to what might otherwise be a difficult problem of equal division: the director of the expedition is required to divide the artifacts into two equal lots and the Directeur General du Service des Antiquités chooses one of them.

For making a survey of possible sites for excavation in Lebanon, three listings of ancient settlements were readily available. The first was a detailed work on the historical topography of Syria and the Lebanon which had been published in 1927 by René Dussaud, an outstanding French scholar conversant with both the ancient and modern sources.[3] Another guide was a compilation of archaeological data from known Lebanese sites published in 1965-1966 by Lorraine Copeland and Peter J. Wescombe.[4] The third source of information, written by Arnulf Kuschke, contains accounts of his surveys of the archaeological sites in the Beqa' Valley, which runs between the Lebanon and the Anti-Lebanon.[5]

Yet even with these excellent guides to more than a hundred sites in Lebanon there remained questions that would have to be answered before the final choice of a site could be made. Was the mound occupied by modern buildings or a cemetery which could not be removed? Could the land be purchased reasonably or rented? Was labor readily available in the area? Where could a staff be

---

[2] *Arêté No. 166 LR du 7 Novembre 1933 portant règlement sur les antiquités*, Haut Commissariat de la Republique Française en Syrie et au Liban, Beyrouth, 1935.

[3] René Dussaud, *Topographie historique de la Syrie antique et médiévale*, 1927, especially maps I, II and V, which cover the Lebanon.

[4] "Inventory of Stone-Age Sites in Lebanon," *Mélanges de l'Université Saint-Joseph*, 41, 1965, pp. 29-175; 42, 1966, pp. 1-174. Although concerned primarily with Neolithic sites the work supplies information on other sites as well.

[5] *Zeitschrift des Deutschen Palästina-Vereins*, 70, 1954, pp. 104-29; 71, 1955, pp. 97-110; 74, 1958, pp. 81-120. R. Hachmann and A. Kuschke, *Bericht über die Ergebnisse der Ausgrabungen in Kamid el-Loz (Libanon) in den Jahren 1963 und 1964*, Saarbrücker Beiträge zur Altertumskunde, 3, 1966, pp. 15-30.

6. Mound at Ras el-Qantara beside the modern fishing harbor

adequately housed? These and other practical considera-tions were involved in making a decision.

We began the survey by exploring sites that lie along the valley of the Euthereus river (modern Nahr el-Kabir), which had been an important ancient trade route between inland Syria and the sea. From sherds picked from the surface it was apparent that three untouched mounds had been occupied extensively in the Bronze Ages: Tell el-Hayat, Tell Biré, and Tell Hmairé. The entire area was virgin territory archaeologically and extremely important historically because of its location along an important line of ancient communication.

The Biqa' Valley was found to be similarly rich in *tells* occupied in the Bronze Ages. Five sites in this fertile valley appeared free of modern encumberance and would have been readily available for excavations: Tell Hizzine, Tell Delhamieh, 'Ain Sherif, Tell el-Jist, and Tell Sirhan. A modern scarp cut into Tell Sirhan revealed stratified layers reaching back into the Early Bronze Age.

Amid so many possibilities it became apparent that a choice would have to be made by criteria other than those we have mentioned. A site that promises to provide entire-ly new historical data was to be preferred. What historical

periods are well documented and what are little known? What major areas of ancient culture are untouched? Here an answer was fairly obvious.

The best known period is by all odds the Roman. Not only Baalbek but scores of sites that display the remains of that flamboyant age of monument builders have been excavated and reconstructed throughout Lebanon. The Hellenistic period is known from M. Dunand's excava-tions at Umm el-'Amed, 19 km. south of Tyre,[6] and what influence the Persians exerted in Lebanon is documented at Amrit and by the spectacular discoveries of M. Dunand at Eshmun, near Sidon.[7]

The most extensively excavated site is Byblos, where the French have worked almost continuously since 1921 and documented the city's history from the Neolithic through the Chalcolithic periods, down to the end of the Bronze Age, as well as in the Persian through the Roman periods. Yet for the period of the Phoenician domination of the coast, roughly from 1200 to 600 B.C., there is a gap in our knowledge of the long history of hu-man occupation.[8] Apart from the famous sarcophagus of Ahiram, little has been found at Byblos to testify to the life of the city during the heyday of the Phoenicians. If

6 M. Dunand et R. Duru, *Oumm el-'Amed: une ville de l'époque hellénistique aux échelles de Tyr*, 1962.
7 For summary and bibliographical references see Nina Jide-

jian, *Sidon through the Ages*, n.d., pp. 59-63.
8 See Nina Jidejian, *Byblos through the Ages*, 1968, pp. 57-59.

there are Iron Age strata at the site, they have not yet been located.

At the historically famous cities of Sidon and Tyre the remains of the Iron Age are inaccessible. The site of Sidon is covered over with the modern buildings of Lebanon's third largest city. Tyre, to be sure, is a principal show-place of archaeological treasures from the Hellenistic and Roman periods. Yet, so spectacular are its public buildings that they cannot be removed to get at the remains that lie beneath.

Thus, in our survey of sites in the summer of 1968, it became increasingly clear that no site on the coast of Lebanon had as yet produced well-stratified evidence of urban occupation in the long period of time from about 1200 to 600 B.C. This obvious gap in the record for the Iron Age occupation along the coast, where Phoenicians had made good use of natural harbors for their maritime enterprises, provided the necessary criterion for narrowing the search for a site. It should be on the coast and bear evidence of occupation during the "dark ages" of the Phoenician period.

There are two coastal sites in the north of Lebanon which had been reported to have been occupied in the Iron Age. Tell Mirhan is situated some 20 km. south of Tripoli within the Bay of Chekka. This small tell, measuring only about 20 by 30 m., had been disfigured in recent years by the cutting of a road which led to the loading platform of a petroleum plant. With the burgeoning of industrial development around the tell and the destruction of part of it, it was apparent that it was already too late to salvage the ancient remains that had accumulated there.

At Sheikh Zennad, 40 km. north of Tripoli, we found also that we had not come soon enough. Large well-cut stones beside the harbor in front of a very low but extensive tell evidenced another port and the sherds could be dated to the Iron Age. But alas, on the very day of our visit a bulldozer was digging out sand to be used in build-ing—and within the scooped-up sand we could see skele-tal remains and pottery which had been placed in the an-cient tombs.

Another possible coastal site was Brak et-Tell, 10 km. south of Sidon. It stands on the seashore, a truncated cone that rises with precipitous sides to a height of from 20 to 25 m.—a textbook example of what a tell should be. But with a top which measures only about 90 by 90 m., it could hardly have been a city of importance. Possibly it had been a fortress, the outer defense of Sidon. Despite the easy availability of the site and its manageable size we judged it an unlikely site for finding the kind of evidence we sought.

Among these and other coastal sites which we explored during the summer of 1968, it was Sarafand that held out the most promise for filling the gap. While it had two good harbors, a name which was probably to be identified with Sarepta, and evidence for extensive occupation in the Roman period, there was an important element missing. Not a single sherd that could be dated to the Iron Age could be discovered either on the surface or in the debris which the sea had dislodged from the *tell*. Yet it was entirely possible that the Iron Age remains were masked by the heavy overlay of later periods of occupation. On the chance that such good harbors would have been utilized by Phoenician sailors we made our decision, for better or for worse, to ask for a concession for six years of excavation. Eventually the President of the Republic of Lebanon issued a decree (No. 15008) which granted the site of Sarafand to the University of Pennsylvania.

Although Sarafand had never been dug before, something was known of its archaeological history. Two museums contained objects which had come, or were said to have come, from the environs of Sarafand. The Louvre possesses a torso from a male statue, decorated with designs that have strong Egyptian affinities; it was purchased by E. G. Rey at Sarafand in 1857 (Fig. 7).[9] The Museum of the American University of Beirut has

what is almost certainly the entire contents of a tomb discovered in the vicinity of the village of Sarafand in 1929.[10] Shortly after the discovery the Museum purchased 67 of the pots and then set about to determine the location of the tomb from which they had been robbed. Three years later Harold Ingholt, then the Director of the Museum, was taken to the reputed source of the discovery and a plan was drawn of the tomb by Eynar Fugmann. Despite the lack of absolute evidence for the provenience of this collection of Late Bronze II pottery (ca. 1400 B.C.) it was to provide useful models in the identification of fragments of Late Bronze Age pottery as they were recovered from the living areas of the excavation.

One more previous discovery should be mentioned. In 1968 Roger Saidah cleaned the soil from some 40 tombs which had been cut in the rocky hills to the east of the coastal road slightly to the north of Sarafand.[11] Although all but three of the tombs had been completely robbed of their burial deposits, the contents of those not plundered indicated that they had been used in the sixth-fifth century B.C. The cemetery probably belonged to the urban settlement along the seashore.

[9] E. G. Rey, *Voyage dans le Haouran*, p. 2, pl. 1.

[10] D. Baramki, *Berytus*, 12, 1956-58, pp. 129-42, pls. 14-16; idem, in *Acts of the International Archaeological Symposium*, "The Mycenaeans in the Eastern Mediterranean," 1973, pp. 193-97.

[11] *Berytus*, 18, 1969, pp. 134-37; Tomb 26 illustrated by W. Culican in *Berytus*, 19, 1970, pp. 15-16, fig. 3.

8. The harbor at Ras esh-Shiq

7. Torso of a statue found at Sarafand in 1857, now in the Louvre

9. Stone blocks protruding from the sand at Ras esh-Shiq

It was clear from our very first visit to Sarafand that the ancient settlement had been spread over a vast area. Where should we begin to excavate in order to find the layers of stratified deposits of ancient habitation that would provide at the very outset a record of human occupation at the site? In all probability the area beside one of the two harbors would have been occupied in any period of major settlement.

The southern harbor at Ras esh-Shiq (Fig. 8) was picked for two reasons. First, the outer edges of three large blocks of worked stone protruded from the sandy beach, suggesting the possibility of a sea wall or quay along the rim of the southern harbor (Fig. 9). Behind this line, if our guess was correct, there should be the remains of the city. Second, the field behind the hypothetical quay was planted in beans, and not in citrus groves, and should be available at a modest rent.

The site had been picked and the location of the initial probe had been determined. On the morning of June 5, 1969, a staff of eight assisted by about 20 workmen began the first excavation to be undertaken at Sarafand. We were curious about any part of the city's past and committed to record as accurately as possible any and all archaeological evidence. But one objective was clear: the recovery of Phoenician remains—if indeed there had been a Phoenician settlement at Sarafand.

II

The Phoenicians: Sources for Their History

WHAT WAS known in 1969 about the history of the Phoenicians and their culture was derived, in large measure, either from written sources or from archaeological excavations made in distant lands where the Phoenicians had planted colonies. There had been no controlled excavation of a city which the Phoenicians had occupied in their homeland. Lacking, therefore, was such basic information as that provided by actual remains of houses, ovens, industrial installations, pots, tools, and other objects of daily life that make possible the reconstruction of a civilization.

Yet, despite this lack of direct archaeological data, much was known. Phoenician inscriptions and a few artifacts which had been discovered on the surface or in tombs provided direct sources of information. Yet most of what we knew about the Phoenicians came from indirect sources, like the writings of contemporary Greeks, Israelites, Assyrians, Egyptians. Since the model of Phoenician culture has been constructed from a variety of sources we should at this point describe the nature of these sources and attempt to assess their value.

The Phoenicians, unlike the Egyptians, Assyrians, or Israelites, for each of whom we have historical annals, are known to us more from what other people recorded about them than from what they themselves wrote. In fact, if we were dependent solely upon surviving Phoenician inscriptions, we would be unaware of the achievements and skills with which they are generally credited in history: the transmission to the West of the alphabet—an invention for storing information efficiently—the first Near Eastern penetration of the Mediterranean for trade and commerce, skill in working metals and carving ivory, and the production of dyed textiles that in time became proverbial as royal or Phoenician purple. For such data about a small but historically significant people we are indebted to others who from time to time mentioned or alluded to the Phoenicians in writing their own literature and histories.

Archaeological testimony, too, comes largely from sites which lie outside the Phoenician homeland. From remains scattered over a large area, from the Tigris in the East to the Atlantic in the West and from North Syria to Egypt, pieces can be fitted together—as one restores an ancient vase from its sherds—to form a composite picture of Phoenician culture. It should occasion no surprise that in joining these pieces of indirect testimony there are problems which, as we shall see presently, have been debated by scholars.

There is no problem, however, about where Phoenicians lived. Most of the cities of the Phoenicians mentioned in ancient texts are known to us, and are located in a coastal strip of less than 200 km. in modern Lebanon, although sometimes Phoenician territory included settlements as far south as Dor, in Palestine, and as far north as al-Mina, on the Syrian coast. The Phoenician cities are located beside good harbors or on islands lying just off shore: Arvad, Byblos, Beirut, Sidon, Sarepta, and Tyre.

General agreement also exists as to the political changes that were taking place in Palestine-Syria toward the end of the second millennium B.C. Well known are the tensions produced by the incursion of new peoples into an area long dominated by independent city states that had shared a common Canaanite culture. Hebrews arrived from the east and conquered parts of Palestine; Philistines and other Sea Peoples settled the fertile plains along the coast of southern Canaan; and Arameans from the northeast came to dominate the hinterland of the Lebanon range. Thus, the Canaanite inhabitants of the littoral of

the Lebanon were cut off from the arable lands to the east which had formerly been in friendly hands. Confined by these newcomers, the Canaanites of the coastal city states, who eventually came to be designated as Phoenicians, found themselves with only the sea as an avenue for trade and an opportunity for expansion. The end of the second millennium witnessed major shifts in population, new alignments, and a significant response to a challenge.

Changes were also taking place in the control of the sea routes. With the destruction of their empire at the end of the thirteenth century, the Mycenaeans lost their maritime trade, for which there is abundant evidence in the form of their distinctive ceramic vessels found throughout the eastern Mediterranean. For a brief period, the Sea Peoples moved into the vacuum; repulsed by the Egyptians, they settled on the coast of Palestine and continued to sail their ships and engage in piratic trade. But their activities were short lived. The time had arrived for the emergence of the Phoenicians as a maritime power.

Actually the very name Phoenician was a term alien to the people to whom it came to be applied. Phoenicians identified themselves by the name Canaanite, the word used widely in the Bible and in other ancient sources for the people of Palestine and Syria. The earliest attested occurrence of the term Canaanite is in a text from the their distinctive product caught on and was widely used by Greek poets and historians, who were to record the achievements of these celebrated seafarers. Yet, had a Sidonian heard the Greek name by which he was to become identified in world history, he probably would not have recognized it as pertaining to him.

Phoenician craftsmanship did not go unnoted by Greek poets. Two brief passages in the *Iliad*, although they describe the heroic days of the Trojan wars, actually reflect the impressions that the Phoenicians made on the Greeks at the end of the eighth century B.C., when the earlier traditions were first put into writing. As a prize for the runners in a foot race at the funeral games for Patroklos, Achilleus set out a mixing-bowl of silver: "for its loveliness it surpassed all others on earth by far, since skilled Sidonian craftsmen had wrought it well, and Phoenicians carried it over the misty face of the water" (23. 742-44, Lattimore trans.) Textiles too were a specialty of Sidon. Paris acquired finely woven garments, "the work of Sidonian women," for Helen when he brought her to Troy (6. 289-92).

Yet in the *Odyssey*, which is slightly later in the date of its composition, the Greek attitude toward the Phoenicians had undergone a change. A man of Phoenicia whom

eighteenth century B.C. recently found at Mari on the Euphrates.[1] In it, Canaanites, along with brigands, are said to have been the residents of an otherwise unknown town of Pahṣum. The name had long currency. More than two thousand years later Augustine recorded that when rustic peasants of Carthage were asked who they were, they would reply, "Canaanites." Apparently the Carthaginians of the fifth century A.D. had kept alive the tradition of their ancient Near Eastern origin.

The Canaanites of the coastal cities were accustomed to refer to themselves more specifically by the name of the city to which they belonged. Sidonian and Tyrian appear in the Phoenician inscriptions, and these names are frequently used in the Old Testament. We may surmise that citizens of other cities were identified by similar terms.

It is to the Greeks that we are indebted for the term Phoenician as well as for other valuable descriptions of their eastern neighbor. The Greek word *phoinix*, which meant among other things, "red-purple or crimson," was used as the name for the people of the eastern Mediterranean coast, presumably because they were well known for their production and use of red dye.[2] This designation of the coastal Canaanites by the name of

[1] *Syria*, 50, 1973, pp. 277-82.
[2] See for the most recent evidence J. D. Muhly, "Homer and

Odysseus encountered in Egypt is described as "well versed in guile, a greedy knave, who had already wrought much evil among men" (14. 288-289, trans. from Loeb ed.). As Rhys Carpenter had pointed out, the erstwhile "craftsmen" had become "craftymen."[3] Admiration for Phoenician skill may have become tempered by a spirit of rivalry and competition for the maritime trade of the Mediterranean.

Writing in the fifth century, Herodotus credited the Phoenicians with two notable achievements: the introduction of the alphabet into Greece (5. 58) and the discovery that the African continent is "encompassed by the sea, save only where it borders on Asia." The story of the first circumnavigation of a continent is told by Herodotus:

... this was proved first (as far as we know) by Necos king of Egypt. He, when he had made an end of digging the canal which leads from the Nile to the Arabian Gulf, sent Phoenicians in ships, charging them to sail on their return voyage past the Pillars of Heracles till they should come into the northern sea and so to Egypt. So the Phoenicians set out from the Red Sea and sailed the southern sea ... so that after two years had passed, it was in the third that they rounded the Pillars of Heracles and came to Egypt (4. 42, trans. from Loeb ed.).

[3] *American Journal of Archaeology*, 62, 1958, p. 36.

The ingenuity of the Phoenician sailors in provisioning their ships during the long voyage is noted by Herodotus. "Whenever autumn came they would put in and sow the land, to whatever part of Libya they might come, and there await the harvest; then, having gathered in the crop, they sailed on."

Other important Greek sources for Phoenician history are quotations that Josephus, the Jewish historian of the first century A.D., made from writings which have not survived. In order to support the authenticity of the biblical stories about Solomon and Hiram of Tyre and the claim for the greater cleverness and learning of the former, Josephus quotes freely from an otherwise unknown author of a "History of the Phoenicians," Dius, and from a Menander of Ephesus (*Against Apion*, 1. 112-26). And in addition to including quotations which supported his own thesis, Josephus generously gave details not found either in the Bible or in other extant sources.

Menander, according to Josephus, credits Hiram of Tyre with the dedication of a golden pillar in the temple of Zeus [*sic*] and the building of new shrines dedicated to Heracles and Astarte; furthermore, from Menander's work Josephus reproduces a list of Tyrian kings, most of whom are not known from other sources. The list is annotated with details about succession, years lived, and years of each reign. Yet in this bare listing of names and years there is little that sheds light on Phoenician culture.

Some information about the Tyrian fleet in the days of Luli (Elulaios, as the name is written in Josephus) and the vulnerability of the island's water supply is supplied in a quotation from Menander. When Tyre would not give in to the Assyrian king, the submissive cities of Sidon, Arka, and Old Tyre supplied him with 60 ships and 800 oarsmen. "Against these," related Menander, "the Tyrians sailed with 12 ships and, after dispersing the ships of their adversaries, took 500 of their men prisoners" (Antiquities, 9. 286-87, trans. from Loeb ed.). In retaliation for this naval defeat of his allies, the Assyrian king "placed guards at the river and the aqueducts to prevent the Tyrians from drawing water, and this they endured for five years, and drank from wells which they had dug." Later we shall have occasion to place this account alongside that of the Assyrian king Sennacherib when he dealt with Luli (see p. 42).

A more direct source consists of inscriptions written by Phoenicians in their own dialect of Canaanite. In the coastal cities of the homeland 64 inscriptions, varying in length from one to 22 lines, have been discovered in the past century and a quarter.[4] If one adds to this listing

those Phoenician inscriptions which have been found in Palestine, Lebanon, Syria, Cilicia, Cyprus, Greece, Egypt, Sardinia, and Spain, then the rather meager sample coming from the homeland is increased by more than five times. Yet, the entire corpus of the principal extant Phoenician inscriptions occupies no more than 13 pages in a recent handbook.[5]

This small but extremely important source of firsthand information can be greatly expanded again by the inclusion of thousands of Punic inscriptions (Phoenician of the sixth-second centuries B.C.) which have been discovered in Carthage and other Punic sites in the West.

Phoenician was the first of the scripts of the forgotten languages of the ancient world to be deciphered and read satisfactorily. On April 12, 1758, the French Abbé J. J. Barthélemy announced to the French Academy his reading of Phoenician inscriptions found on Malta and Cyprus.[6] The inscription from Cyprus had been copied by the English traveler Richard Pococke when he visited Kition in the fall of 1738—he had been at Sarepta in May of that year and, as we shall see later, recorded some observations about the antiquities of the site. Pococke patiently copied three lines of characters which he could

4 F. L. Benz, *Personal Names in the Phoenician and Punic Inscriptions*, 1972, pp. 15-28.

5 H. Donner and W. Röllig, *Kanaanäische und Aramäische Inschriften*, Band 1: Texte, 1966, pp. 1-13.

6 *Mémoires de l'Académie Royale des Inscriptions et Belles-Lettres*, 30, 1758, pp. 405-27.

discern on a white marble plaque that measured 10 by 30 cm. Twenty years later Barthélemy read most of the letters correctly from Pococke's copy. Later, in 1766, with the aid of a new copy of the Kition inscription, which had by this time been deposited in the Bodleian Library at Oxford, he was able to produce a reading which, except for two out of the 78 letters, is correct. Now the Phoenician scripts are well documented, and the modern student is as well provided with grammars and lexicons of Phoenician as he is for other languages of the ancient Near East.

Although this extensive body of written material is now adequately read, it is severely restricted in the scope of its subject matter. There are some building and sepulchral inscriptions, a few texts which are concerned with the cult and sacrifices, incantations, an important treaty; but the largest number by far are simple dedicatory texts, devoting a stela to a deity. Thousands of examples of the latter type are known from Carthage alone. If one compares the collection of Phoenician texts with the broad documentation of ancient life preserved in the corpus of cuneiform documents, containing as they do business and legal documents, historical annals, laws, myths, epics, songs, one is aware of the limitation of the Phoenician sources. They are almost exclusively monumental in char-

acter, displays to be seen and read by men and the gods, with little about daily activities and the commerce for which the Phoenicians were famous.

Limited though they are to a narrow segment of human concern, Phoenician inscriptions provide a vast repertory of names, in a few cases those of kings, but mostly names borne by otherwise unknown people, both men and women.

These proper names consist of a phrase or short sentence containing the name of a deity. Thus the name Eshmunyaton found on a fragment of a bowl at Sarepta (p. 102) means "Eshmun has given," and Germelqart (p. 98) signifies "Client of Melqart." The divine elements of proper names may provide a clue to the popularity of the god worshiped at a particular place or in a certain period of time.

In 1795 there was found in Athens an inscription which mentions a 'Abdtanit, "Servant of Tanit," who is said to be a Sidonian.[7] Since the goddess Tanit had until recently been known only from Carthage, it had long been assumed that 'Abdtanit was a Carthaginian who had migrated to Greece. In 1974, however, we found the name of the well-known Carthaginian goddess Tanit on an inscription within the shrine at Sarepta, where she was worshiped (p. 105) 'Abdtanit may then have been a Sidonian after all.

7 H. Donner and W. Röllig, Kanaanäische und Aramäische Inschriften, Band II: Kommentar, 1968, no. 53.

10. Lid from the sarcophagus of Ahiram, with representations of King Ahiram (right) and his son, Ittoba'l (left)

Kings of Phoenician city states were given extravagant burials, which were often safeguarded with dire threats to robbers. Typical of the curses incised on the tombs is the famous text on the sarcophagus of Ahiram, found at Byblos in 1923 and now the principal treasure of the National Museum in Beirut. A translation reads:

A sarcophagus made by [It]toba'l, the son of Ahiram, king of Byblos, for Ahiram, his father, as his eternal (dwelling-) place. If there be a king among kings and a governor among governors and an army commander up in Byblos who shall uncover this sarcophagus, let his judicial staff be broken, let his royal throne be upset! May peace flee from Byblos, and he himself be wiped out! (ANET³, 661).

Besides bearing the oldest extensive Phoenician inscription known, the Ahiram sarcophagus is important for yet another reason. The reliefs which decorate its sides and lid are rare examples of early Phoenician art. Carved on the lid and decorated with red and blue paint is the figure of the deceased king with his hand upraised in a gesture of benediction upon his son, who stands facing him (Fig. 10). It has been suggested that this is the earliest portrait of a father and son on a monument of Western Asia. Between the royal figures are two lions,

11. King Ahiram of Byblos seated on a sphinx throne before an offering table and server, on the side of the sarcophagus

11). Four crouching lions support the sarcophagus. Rarely has a single artifact preserved such a wealth of detail about clothing, hair styles, furniture, and funerary customs of an ancient people.

Since the discovery of the Ahiram sarcophagus by Pierre Montet, its date has been a matter of controversy. Tight lines of argument have been drawn between the advocates of a thirteenth-century date and those who assign it to the tenth century—a singular discrepancy of three centuries.

The sarcophagus was discovered along with two others, neither one decorated, in a semicircular tomb chamber about 8 m. below the surface of the rock. On one wall of the vertical shaft, about 4 m. square, leading down to the tomb appeared a laconic warning in Phoenician: "Attention! Behold, thou shalt come to grief below here!"[8]

The upper 4 m. of the shaft contained pottery as late in date as the Hellenistic or Roman period and sherds which could be dated to a time as early as the fourteenth century B.C. Obviously the fill was late and composed of mixed materials. Below this fill the excavators encountered sterile earth, but at the bottom of the shaft and within the burial chamber there appeared what seemed to be firm evidence for dating: fragments of alabaster vessels inscribed with the names of the famous thirteenth-century

shown tail to tail and with their heads projecting menacingly beyond the edge of the sarcophagus.

The four sides of the sarcophagus are profusely decorated with mourners, attendants, offering bearers, and the departed king himself sitting majestically on a sphinx throne before a table spread with offering of food (Fig.

[8] Translation of W. F. Albright, *Journal of the American Oriental Society*, 67, 1947, p. 156.

Egyptian king Ramses II. It seemed that the archaeologists had been preceded into the tomb chamber by robbers, who in their looting had discarded these broken alabaster treasures as well as a broken ivory plaque carved with a battle scene between a griffin and a lion. The Ramses II vessels had been tomb goods buried with the thirteenth-century Ahiram—or so at least it seemed to the excavators.[9] Thus by excellent archaeological logic both the writing and the carving on the sarcophagus were placed securely in time. This conclusion, however, was soon to be challenged.

The first attack upon the thirteenth-century date came from the paleographers, who compared the forms of certain Phoenician letters of the inscription with those of other inscriptions of clearly established dates. One of these, found at Byblos, was an epigraph of Abibaal, which could be dated to the tenth century since it appeared on the fragment of a statue of the Egyptian king Shishak. The other was that of Elibaal, incised on a torso of Osorkon I, who began his reign in Egypt at the end of the tenth century. Strong similarities between the script of the Ahiram sarcophagus on the one hand and that of the two closely dated inscriptions on the other led the American

orientalist W. F. Albright to argue convincingly in 1947 for a date about three centuries later than that proposed by the excavators.[10]

Yet other aspects of the Ahiram sarcophagus could not be neglected: the style and iconography of the reliefs on the lid and the sides. Comparisons were made with such carvings as that on a thirteenth-twelfth century ivory found at Megiddo, Assyrian representations from the time of the ninth-century Shalmaneser III and other well dated examples of ancient Near Eastern art. In summing up the case made from the approach of art history, Edith Porada came to the conclusion in 1973 that a date of 1000 B.C., or slightly later, would best fit the comparative evidence. In a reconstruction of the history of the use of the tomb chamber in the tenth century she concluded that the thirteenth-century tomb "was cleaned, not too carefully . . . and some of the fragments remained on the floor inside the chamber, while others were dropped in the shaft—and then the sarcophagus of Ahiram was introduced into the chamber."[11] The date of the most important single monument of Phoenician history continues to be a subject of debate among scholars.

Sources written by the Egyptians that describe their

[9] Pierre Montet, *Byblos et l'Égypte*, 1928, pp. 215-38.
[10] W. F. Albright, *Journal of the American Oriental Society*, 67, 1947, p. 154.

[11] *The Journal of the Ancient Near Eastern Society of Columbia University*, 5, 1973, p. 363.

contacts with the peoples of the Phoenician cities during the twelfth through the seventh centuries are limited to a single document, a papyrus purchased in Cairo in 1890 by the Russian Egyptologist Wladimir Golénischeff, and now deposited in the Moscow Museum. It is a story of the misadventures of Wen-Amon, an emissary from the Temple of Amon at Karnak, who was sent to Byblos to procure timber for the bark of the god Amon-Re (ANET³, 25-29). Obviously the narrative is a literary composition, in which its author makes good use of suspense, irony, and sarcasm, yet so true are the references to what we know from other sources for the history of the eleventh century B.C. that it has been characterized as "the literary version of an actual report by an Egyptian official."¹² As to this appraisal of its authenticity there is general agreement.

Most instructive is the picture which it presents of maritime activity in Phoenician ports at the beginning of the eleventh century. The Tjeker, one of the well-known Peoples of the Sea, were in control of the seaport of Dor on the Palestinian coast, but Phoenician ports bristled with maritime activity, even though they were menaced by the Tjeker.

The papyrus provides details about such subjects as the location of the palace of the prince of Byblos, the political

structure of the city state and religious practices. Zakar-Baal, the prince, is described in a kind of optical illusion as "sitting (in) his upper room, with his back turned to a window, so that the waves of the great Syrian sea broke against the back of his head." The Prince depended on one occasion for counsel, or possibly legal opinion, on an "assembly" (cf. *mô'ēd*, a word used in the Hebrew Bible for "assembly"). At one crucial stage of the mission, when Wen-Amon despaired of getting the timber for which he had been sent, the Prince was influenced to provide it by an oracle spoken by a frenzied youth, apparently a court page who had charismatic powers of prophecy. This is the earliest reference in ancient Near Eastern writings to the kind of religious phenomenon which was to become characteristic of the earlier Hebrew prophets.

In payment for the timber which Wen-Amon eventually received, the Egyptians paid in commodities which were needed in Phoenicia. The inventory includes:

4 jars and 1 *kak-men* of gold; 5 jars of silver; 10 pieces of clothing in royal linen; 10 *kherd* of good Upper Egyptian linen; 500 (rolls of) finished papyrus; 500 cowhides; 500 ropes; 20 sacks of lentils; and 30 baskets of fish (ANET³, 28).

These details from an adventure story of the hapless Wen-Amon, who in spite of being robbed on his way from Tanis to Byblos and being treated with persistent contempt by Zakar-Baal, finally got the timber and sailed for home, enrich the record of what we know of Byblos in the eleventh century.

The general impression one gets of the Phoenicians from reading the Old Testament—there are more than a hundred references to Sidon, Tyre, Arvad, or Byblos—is that they were respected neighbors with whom Israel was able to maintain amicable diplomatic and commercial relations throughout a span of a half millennium. This record of peaceful coexistence is surprising when one recalls the wars that the Israelites waged with Philistines, Arameans, Ammonites, Moabites, and the hostile raids upon Israel by Egyptians, Assyrians, and Babylonians. Yet despite the ideological differences between Israel and her northern neighbors, détente prevailed.

In the Hebrew writings, as in the Homeric literature, there are allusions to the celebrated Phoenician skills and occupations. Sidonians and Tyrians are "merchants . . . that pass over the sea," experts in hewing timber, rowers and pilots, and the makers of decks of larch wood inlaid with ivory (Isa. 23:2; I Kings 5:20; Ez. 27:8, 6). Tyre in particular appears in the poetic literature as the ideal of a rich, prosperous, and beautiful city (Isa. 23:8; Amos 1:10; Zech. 9:3; Ez. 27:3). Although Sidon is respected, it could not be forgotten that her goddess was Ashtart, a name the Israelite scribe wrote with the five consonants 'štrt, and vocalized them by the vowels of the familiar Hebrew word for "shame," making the Sidonian goddess appear in the bastard form Ashtoreth.

Besides these general allusions to the Phoenicians, the Bible provides details of specific contacts. Solomon is said to have made a contract with the Tyrian king Hiram (I Kings 5:26). For a fixed annual payment of wheat and beaten oil, Hiram provided cedar and cypress timber, which was made into rafts, towed from the port in Lebanon to a Palestinian port, and from thence brought overland to Jerusalem, where the wood was used in the building of the temple. Large labor forces of Solomon worked in the Lebanon and "Solomon's builders and Hiram's builders and the men of Byblos (Gebalites) did fashion them, and prepared the timber and the stones to build the house" (I Kings 5:32). The Phoenician involvement went even further. An expert in working bronze, also bearing the name of Hiram, was brought from Tyre to cast the bronze appointments for the Jerusalem temple (I Kings 7:13-14). It is difficult to know how much historical truth has been preserved in these stories. We do not have the primary source from which they are said to have been taken, a document called "The Book of the Acts of Solomon"

(1 Kings 11:41). It has long been recognized that the section of 1 Kings 3-11 is a religious history written with a strong polemical bias several centuries after the time of Solomon, whose wisdom and greatness are clearly the dominant themes of the compiler. The oriental hyperbole and flattery in the speeches which are attributed to both Solomon and Hiram (this king from Melqart's city of Tyre says: "blessed be Yahweh this day, who hath given David a wise son . . ."—1 Kings 5:21) suggest later embellishment. There are the improbable figures of tens of thousands of hewers of wood, a figure which seems excessive for a force to procure timber for a building which is later described as measuring 20 by 60 cubits (11 by 32 m.). Furthermore, Hiram is not mentioned in any of the extrabiblical sources (except that of Josephus, who was dependent here on the biblical narrative). Despite these questions, which seem legitimate in appraising these colorful narratives as history, it would seem reasonable to conclude that the king of Tyre did exploit commercially his resources in timber and the skill of his craftsmen in a time of cordial relations with his southern neighbor Israel.

Belonging to the same indirect and secondary source in the biblical history of Solomon's reign are traditions that concern Sidonian trade on the Mediterranean and the Red Sea. Hiram is said to have sent sailors to man the ships of Solomon's navy (1 Kings 9:26-27), and his own ships

are said to have sailed with Solomon's Tarshish fleet, bringing once every three years "gold, and silver, ivory, and apes, and peacocks" (1 Kings 10:22). It is impossible to tell from the text of these stories of Phoenician seamanship whether they reflect impressions gained in the tenth century, to which Solomon belonged, or if the descriptions are more pertinent to the seventh century, when the narratives were probably cast in their present form.

Diplomatic and cultural relations between Israel and the Sidonians seem to have been strengthened by a royal marriage. Ahab, king of Israel in Samaria, took as a wife Jezebel, the daughter of Ethbaal (Ittobaal, "Baal is with him"), king of the Sidonians (1 Kings 16:31). The colorful popular stories about Elijah and his contests with the Phoenician cult of Baal and Asherah (1 Kings 18:19) supply evidence at least for the extensive following which the prophets of that cult could claim even in northern Israel. Apart from the reported practice of self-laceration by the Phoenician prophets—"they cried aloud, and cut themselves after their manner with swords and lances, until the blood gushed out upon them" (1 Kings 18:28)—nothing in the accounts describes the Phoenician cult.

Colorful as these biblical stories are, their worth as trustworthy sources for a history of Phoenicia is severely restricted by the obvious nationalistic and religious purposes which they serve in the composition of which they are a part. As yet archaeological sources are lacking for any details of the Solomonic buildings in Jerusalem, to which Phoenician workmen are said to have contributed their skills. The name of Hiram is mentioned only in the Bible and sources dependent upon it. Yet there is reflected in this view of Phoenicia certain general impressions. The Phoenicians were expert sailors, skilled workmen in stone, wood, and metal; and they were, above all, men of commerce and trade who exploited their resources in timber and labor for profit.

In contrast to the anecdotal nature of the record of Israel's contacts with the Phoenician cities as preserved in the Book of Kings stands the formality of reports by Assyrian kings on their campaigns to exact tribute. For the most part the annals consist of lists of the cities that paid tribute willingly or were looted, but occasionally the monotony of these lists is broken by the inclusion of a detail that sheds light on the history and culture of the subject city, names its king, or enumerates products taken as booty. In addition to these records, which were frequently displayed on monuments in the capital to satisfy the king's vanity and increase his reputation at home, there are graphic representations on stone and in bronze of events which took place on a campaign to the Phoenician coast. The first Assyrian king to push westward to the Lebanon

was Tiglath-pileser I (1114-1076 B.C.). He boasted that he conquered the entire country of the West and collected tribute from Byblos, Sidon, and Arvad. He went into the mountains and cut cedar beams for the temple of Anu and Adad. He ventured on the high sea, where he "killed a narwhal which they call 'seahorse'" (ANET³, 275). After this laconic record of exploitation and adventure, Assyrian annals fail us for two centuries.

When Assyrian supremacy was reestablished in the ninth century, kings began again to exploit the natural resources and prosperity of the coastal cities. No less than eight Assyrian kings—among them the most famous, Ashurnasirpal II, Shalmaneser III, Tiglath-pileser III, Sargon, Sennacherib, Esarhaddon, Ashurbanipal—left records of their campaigns over the two and a half centuries during which Assyria was the major power in the Near East. The Assyrian "yoke" of taxation seems to have been worn patiently for over a century. With Sargon II (721-705) there appear the first signs of revolt, and by the time of Esarhaddon (680-669) discontent reached such proportions in Sidon that this king was obliged to destroy the city and build another, which he populated with peoples from other regions.

In addition to naming the city from which tribute was received, the annals frequently provide the name of the ruler of the city. The syllabic signs of the Akkadian cuneiform in which the Assyrian records are written present in a different guise the sentence names we are accustomed to see in alphabetic form, such as *Ma-ta-an-ba-ʾal*, MTNBʾL, "Gift of Baal"; *U-ru-mil-ki*, ʾRMLK, "Milk is light"; *A-zi-baʿal*, ʾZBʾL, "Baal is strength." Frequently Assyrian sources supply names of Phoenician kings which do not appear in any other sources. The care with which the scribes recorded names of Phoenician rulers increases the credibility of other of their observations, such as the kinds of tribute received.

Ashurnasirpal II (883-859) provided a list of the kinds of tribute received from Tyre, Sidon, Byblos, and Arvad, as well as from the less familiar Mahallata, Maiza, and Kaiza, in an inventory that represents what must have been the stock-in-trade of Phoenician merchants: Gold, silver, tin, copper, copper containers, linen garments with multicolored trimmings, . . . ebony, boxwood, ivory from walrus tusks (*ANET*³, 276).

Diplomatic relations were cordial between the Phoenician cities and Ashurnasirpal II, to judge from a text discovered in 1951 describing the feast which the king gave in Calah, his capital, on the occasion of the opening of the royal palace. Among the 69,574 guests invited to the banquet were delegates from Tyre and Sidon (*ANET*³, 560). When Shalmaneser III (858-824), the son and succes-

sor to Ashurnasirpal II, received tribute from Tyre he was not content with leaving only a written account. His artists depicted on a copper band, which decorated the door of a great gate at Balawat, a scene of the Assyrian king receiving the tribute which was being ferried from the Island of Tyre to the mainland (Fig. 12).[13] That there be no mistake about the identity of the city the repoussé band bore the label: "I received the tribute (brought) on ships from the inhabitants of Tyre and Sidon" (*ANET*³, 281).

Tyre is pictured as built on an island surrounded by crenelated walls and towers. Boats with an animal head on bow and stern are being pulled up to the mainland by ropes as bearded Tyrian porters clad in long, sleeveless garments and wearing pointed, tight-fitting caps, unload a varied cargo, consisting of ingots of metal, cauldrons, trays filled with small objects (possibly carved ivory work), and other small objects carefully cupped in the hands of the porters. Assyrian officers present the tribute to the king, who is followed by a retinue of officers, cavalry, and chariots emerging from a military camp on the mainland of Tyre.

In this unique picture of Tyrians and their products there is a noticeable absence of bound captives and the corpses of resisters, both of which are represented in the scene immediately below depicting the attack upon Hazazu. Presumably the Tyrians were too practical to offer resist-

[13] James B. Pritchard, *The Ancient Near East in Pictures*, 2nd ed., 1969, (hereafter ANEP²), 356-61, upper register.

12. Tribute taken from Tyre by Shalmaneser III, depicted on the bronze gates of Balawat

ance to the powerful Assyrian army or the Assyrians too calculating in their desire for more booty from such a prosperous state to put the inhabitants of Tyre to death.

A letter discovered in 1952 as a part of a collection of over 300 clay tablets of a royal archive in the Assyrian capital at Calah, the modern Nimrud, written by a certain Qurdi-ashshur-lamur, who had been placed by the king (probably Tiglath-pileser III) in Tyre and Sidon to tax the trade in timber exported from the Lebanon, provides us with a vivid picture of the problems the Assyrians encountered as they sought to exact tribute. The official detailed his troubles to the king:

Concerning the people of Tyre . . . all the *wharves are occupied by the people.* Its subjects (i.e. those of Tyre) who are within them (i.e. the wharves) enter (and) leave the warehouses, give (and) receive (in barter), ascend (and) descend Mount Lebanon . . . as they will (and) they have timber brought down here. I exact a tax (on it from) those who have timber brought down. (As to) the tax-collectors (who were) over the wharves of Mount Lebanon, *the people of Tyre attacked and killed* (them). I then appointed, when he came down to me, a tax-collector who (had been) in the warehouses of Sidon. The Sidonians then attacked him. Thereupon I sent the Itu'a contingent to Mount Lebanon: they made the people jump around![14]

[14] Translation by H.W.F. Saggs in *Iraq*, 17, 1955, pp. 127-28, (italics indicate uncertainty of translation).

When the rebellion had been put down, Qurdi-ashshur-lamur gave an order to the Sidonian workmen: "Henceforth have timber brought down here, do your work upon (it), (but) do not sell it to the Egyptians (or) to the Palestinians." Assyria seemed to have been in complete control of the commercial activities of the Phoenicians.

By the time of Sargon II (721-705) there appeared the first intimation of revolt. Hopeful of relief from Assyrian "taxation," the king of Arvad joined forces with other rulers of Syrian cities and Samaria in Palestine. Sargon met them at Qarqar and defeated them, reporting, "the rebels I killed in their cities and established (again) peace and harmony" (ANET³, 285).

Sennacherib has provided us with what is the best documentation for the appearance of Phoenician ships and a picture of what is probably the city of Tyre on two panels which were discovered in Nineveh over a century ago. Although the sculptured reliefs have disappeared, drawings of them have been preserved. One was published by A. H. Layard in 1848; the other, depicting a prominent building within a walled city from which a ship receives embarking passengers, is an original sketch made by Layard which had remained in the files of the British Museum unpublished. In 1956 R. D. Barnett recognized that these two scenes had originally been parts of a single scene, which, he argued

15 R. D. Barnett in *Archaeology*, 9, 1956, p. 93.

convincingly, depicted the flight of the Sidonian King Luli and his family from Tyre in 701 B.C. (Fig. 13)15 (see p. 42 for the text). Within the crenelated walls of Tyre stands a building with a doorway flanked by two columns surmounted by capitals of floral decoration. These two pillars recall to mind the observation of Herodotus when he visited Tyre some three centuries after Sannacherib's time. He recorded: "There I saw it [the temple of Heracles], richly equipped with many other offerings, besides that in it there were two pillars, one of refined gold, one of emerald, a great pillar that shone in the night-time" (2. 44, trans. Loeb ed.).

The sea into which the ship at the quay is about to sail is filled with two distinct types of vessels. The craft at the dock—and five others like it to the left—is a bireme with the bow and stern similarly rounded. Compartments for the two rows of oarsmen are shown below a deck surrounded by a screen on which shields are hung. Among the passengers appears an occasional soldier armed with bow or spear.

Interspersed among these passenger vessels are ships of different design. A ram projects to a sharp point at the bow and the ship is equipped with a mast and single sail attached to the yard, and a superstructure similarly hung with rounded shields. This type of naval vessel has a long

13. Flight of King Luli from Tyre, pictured on a relief of Sennacherib found at Nineveh

history reaching back into sub-Mycenaean times in Greece.[16] So impressed was Sennacherib with Phoenician skill in seamanship that he took a contingent of Tyrian, Sidonian, and Cyprian sailors across the desert to the Tigris.[17]

It was not until the third decade of the seventh century that the Assyrians experienced any effective resistance to their periodic raids upon the coastal cities. Esarhaddon was compelled to use more than the usual show of force to obtain his tribute. He boasted that he "leveled all its [Sidon's] urban buildings," "tore up and cast into the sea its walls and its foundations" (ANET[3], 290). He caught her king Abdimilkutte in the open sea like a fish, took his head as a trophy of war, and paraded with it through the wide main street of Nineveh in order to "demonstrate to the population the power of Ashur," his god (ANET[3], 291). As for Tyre, the island city, he resorted to starving out its inhabitants to effect his purpose: "I withheld from them food and (fresh) water which sustains life." In addition he forced the unlucky victims to transport, "under terrible difficulties," wood to be used for building material at Nineveh, his capital.

Thus the coastal cities learned the futility of resistance. Esarhaddon's successor Ashurbanipal continued to make expeditions, but Sidon is not mentioned. Tyre, however, had to be starved out again and Arvad's king perished; his sons surrendered and one was picked to be installed as king.

The rich archive for Phoenician history which the Assyrian annals provide is replete with details of tribute, sieges, the names of kings, atrocities, deportations. Conspicuously absent, however, is the record of everyday life, so familiar to the writers of contemporary cuneiform documents that it was not deemed worth recording. Only an occasional relief in bronze or stone depicting a siege, looting, or attack has survived.

Among the archaeological sources which were available before the Sarepta excavations for the history of Phoenician culture are the ceramic vessels found in tombs in Phoenicia proper. The largest single collection of pots belongs to the National Museum in Beirut. It consists of 317 vessels known with reasonable certainty—some were actually confiscated from grave looters at the site—to have come from four cemeteries in South Lebanon, located at Khirbet Silm, Joya, Qasmieh, and Qrayé.[18] These cemeteries lie near

[16] R. D. Barnett, "Early Shipping in the Near East," Antiquity, 32, 1958, pp. 220-230; Lucien Basch, "Phoenician Oared Ships," The Mariner's Mirror, 55, 1969, pp. 139-62, 227-45.

[17] D. D. Luckenbill, Ancient Records of Assyria and Babylonia, 1926-1927, II, par. 319.

[18] Berytus, 21, 1972, pp. 55-194.

enough to Tyre and Sidon to reflect the culture that we term Phoenician.

From certain decorative features of the jugs in this collection of funerary pottery, which has been dated roughly to the tenth through the eighth centuries B.C., it is apparent that similar forms were also made from bronze. On the neck of some jugs there is a horizontal ridge which serves no functional purpose; yet, on a metal prototype the band around the neck would have functioned to secure the upper end of the handle. On other of the ceramic jugs pellets of clay are attached to the body of the vessel either at each side of the point of attachment of the handle or below it. They would seem to be representations of the rivets that were used on the metal prototype. Furthermore, a ridge at the base of the neck may well simulate the join between the neck and body of a metal jug. With the reputation which the Phoenicians had for working metal it is no surprise to find in the cemeteries of South Lebanon this indirect evidence for their celebrated craftsmanship. Apparently an imitation in pottery sufficed in these burial deposits.

Another important group of funerary pottery has come from a carefully controlled excavation made by Roger Saidah at Khaldé, on the coast just south of Beirut.[19] There the 11 representative burials, containing 61 vessels,

[19] *Bulletin du Musée de Beyrouth*, 19, 1966, pp. 51-90.

have been assigned to two periods of interment: an earlier that extended from the tenth to the end of the ninth century, and a later which covered the period from the end of the ninth to the end of the eighth century B.C.

It was apparent, however, that these two important collections of Iron Age pottery were not representative of the total ceramic production of Phoenician potters. Almost totally lacking are the containers and utensils of everyday life, such as the widely used storage jar, which we were to find in such quantities at Sarepta, and the ordinary cooking pot.

Although the kind of documentation for the Iron Age that comes from the stratified layers of urban occupation has been lacking for the Phoenician homeland, excavations both to the north and to the south have thrown light on certain elements of Phoenician culture as it spread to these regions. Soundings made by Leonard Woolley at al-Mina, a port on the Bay of Sueidia, where the Orontes empties into the Mediterranean, have clarified the origin and the dating of certain well-known wares which were once vaguely labelled as Cypro-Phoenician. Joan du Plat Taylor, who published a study of the Cypriot and Syrian pottery found at the site, was able to demonstrate that two distinctive wares (red-slip and black-on-red) originated on the Phoenician coast and then spread to Cyprus.[20] At Tell Sukas, 26

[20] *Iraq*, 21, 1959, p. 88.

km. south of Latakia, pottery recognized as Phoenician has been discovered both in the soundings of 1934 and in the five seasons of work from 1958 to 1963, during which systematic excavations were carried out by F. J. Riis.[21]

Along the coast south of Tyre four cemeteries have been found to contain pottery that attests the spread of Phoenician culture: Tell er-Rashidiyeh, 7 km. south of Tyre;[22] ez-Zib (Achzib);[23] Mt. Carmel, near Haifa;[24] and Athlit.[25] In addition to these burials, stratified evidence for the Phoenician period has been recovered in Level III of the site of Tell Abu Hawam, situated on the Bay of Acco between Mt. Carmel and the river Kishon.[26] Although all of these sites lie outside the boundaries of Phoenicia proper, they have contributed something to our knowledge of the center from which Phoenician styles and techniques spread.

It is not surprising that articles of Phoenician craftsmanship should have been identified at places far distant from the homeland of a people who were celebrated for their trade and commerce. Cyprus, Carthage, Sicily, Sardinia, Andalusia, and even the Atlantic coast of Morocco have provided clear evidence for Phoenician cultural penetration in the form of Phoenician inscriptions as well as of numerous artifacts that display styles and motifs that relate them to the Levantine homeland.

Most conspicuous among items of Phoenician origin found at sites around the edge of the Mediterranean, and even in Mesopotamia, are carved ivories and decorated metal bowls. From the Northwest palace at Nimrud on the Upper Tigris there has come a collection of ivory inlays for furniture, which have, in addition to Phoenician letters incised on their backs—presumably to aid the workmen in fitting the ivories into wood—motifs and designs that point to a Phoenician origin.[27] Arslan Tash, a site in the Upper Euphrates area, and Samaria, the well-known biblical site in Palestine, have added ivories inspired by models found in the cities of the Lebanese coast even if they were not manufactured there.

In view of the Homeric reference to the beautiful Si-

[21] A.M.H. Ehrich, *Early Pottery in the Jebeleh Region*, 1939; F. J. Riis, *Sūkās* 1, 1970.

[22] *Revue Biblique*, 1904, pp. 564-70; *Bulletin du Musée de Beyrouth*, 6, 1942-1943, p. 86.

[23] Unpublished except for short notices. See *Palestine Exploration Quarterly*, 1948, p. 88; *Revue Biblique*, 1960, p. 398; 1962, pp. 404-05; etc.

[24] *Bulletin of the British School of Archaeology in Jerusalem*, no. 5, pls. 2 and 3, pp. 47-55.

[25] *Quarterly of the Department of Antiquities in Palestine*, 6, 1938, pp. 121-52.

[26] *Quarterly of the Department of Antiquities in Palestine*, 3, 1933, pp. 74-80; 4, 1935, pp. 1-69.

[27] R. D. Barnett, *A Catalogue of the Nimrud Ivories*, 1957, pp. 111-53.

donian bowl (p. 17) and the biblical tradition about Hiram, the metal-worker from Tyre (p. 25), it is surprising that no decorated metal bowls have come from Phoenicia proper. Numerous examples, however, have been found elsewhere. Assyria (Nimrud), Cyprus, Greece, Etruria are areas which have yielded examples from the ninth and eighth centuries of bronze or silver bowls that display Phoenician art and craftsmanship. While the artists have drawn upon Egyptian and Assyrian iconography for their compositions, they have, nevertheless, portrayed these borrowed features in styles which are distinctively Phoenician.[28] Inscriptions on some of the bowls lend additional support to a claim for Phoenician origin. These representations upon the bowls, when combined with those from the ivories, constitute the major source for what may be called Phoenician art.

We may summarize the sources for the history of the Phoenicians in the cities of their homeland by listing the data which they provide according to three broad categories. First, skills and commercial activities of the Phoenicians—navigation, maritime commerce, dyed textiles, and the exploitation of their natural resource of timber—are mentioned in the writings of the Greeks, Israelites, and Egyptians. The broad lines of these activities are drawn by a phrase or other casual reference in such a variety of independent sources that the credibility of the general picture of the delineation of Phoenician culture can hardly be challenged.

The second category of sources provides more specific evidence, but it is limited in its scope: the names of kings and events of national importance found in the Phoenician inscriptions, Assyrian annals, and sources we have only at second hand, such as the writings of Dius, Menander, and "The Book of the Acts of Solomon." For the most part the information deals with rulers, succession, foreign relations, and matters which were of concern only indirectly to Phoenician craftsmen and merchants.

It is the third category of evidence that provides a documentation for the everyday life. In the few surviving pictures carved on stone or hammered in bronze there is a record of cultural detail which was taken for granted by those who wrote and then was lost as cultural patterns changed. With the discovery of artifacts in tombs the picture of Phoenician life is brought more closely into focus, but even these objects chosen for the specialized purpose of serving the dead are an inadequate measure of the culture of the living. From peripheral areas, both on the coast and in areas where the Phoenicians traded or founded

The Art and Architecture of the Ancient Orient, 1954, pp. 195-201.

[28] Phoenician elements have been noted by S. Moscati, *The World of the Phoenicians*, 1968, pp. 66-75, and by H. Frankfort,

THE PHOENICIANS: SOURCES FOR THEIR HISTORY

colonies, there has come testimony to their craftsmanship in ivory and metal.

It was in this context of available sources that we began our excavations at Sarafand. Our aim was to reconstruct, as far as possible, through controlled archaeological investigation the material culture of the Phoenicians in their homeland—a perspective which heretofore had not been adequately provided by the existing sources.

III

Sarepta in Tradition and History

When one surveys the sources for the history of the Phoenician cities it is obvious that Tyre, Sidon, Byblos, and Arvad are those most frequently mentioned. Sarepta is less prominent in the record. Yet the appearance of the name of the city in ancient Egyptian, Assyrian, Hebrew, and Greek documents of various dates can provide a framework for its history.

In the eyes of the Western world, however, Sarepta enjoyed a prominence throughout more than a millennium which not even Tyre and Sidon could match. As early as the fourth century A.D., Christian pilgrims from Europe began to visit the site where, according to the Bible, Elijah had sojourned with the widow and performed two of his most spectacular miracles.

The account of the Hebrew prophet's visit to Sarepta (Zarephath) has survived in a rich collection of folk stories about him in the First Book of Kings, a document that is primarily a religious history, avowedly partisan to the cult of Yahweh, god of Israel. The language is that of the street and market place, not that of an archive of historical records. Strictly plebeian in its concerns for food in time of famine and for the life of the only child of a poor widow, the story was destined to have a wide appeal to the peasants, who knew only too well the realities of starvation, widowhood, and fatal sickness.

Chapter 17 of I Kings tells of a poor widow's kindness to an imperious stranger, who, as it turned out, was none other than a prophet, capable of working miracles for her during a severe famine in both Israel and Phoenicia. Arriving at the city gate of Sarepta, thirsty and hungry, Elijah demanded some water and then bread from a widow as she gathered wood to bake what she thought was to be a last meal. When the widow hesitated to share her remaining flour and oil with a stranger, the prophet reassured her that, "the jar of meal shall not be spent, and the cruse of oil shall not fail, until the day that Yahweh sends rain upon the earth." And an undiminishing supply of oil and flour sustained both the family and the prophet, who was lodged in an upper room of the house until the end of the famine.

A second miracle demonstrated that in addition to producing the sustenance for life Elijah could provide life itself.

14. Painting of Elijah restoring the life of the widow's son at Sarepta, from the synagogue at Dura-Europos

When the son of the widow became ill—"his illness was so severe that there was no breath left in him"—Elijah carried the child up to his room, stretched himself on him three times, and asked Yahweh to restore his life. "The soul of the child came into him again," the account goes, and Elijah brought him down from the upper chamber and delivered him to his mother, who acknowledged the prophet's authority.

This dramatic story from the ninth century B.C. became in time a classic. A Jewish synagogue built at Dura-Europos on the Euphrates in the third century A.D. was decorated with a mural that depicted in vivid colors the raising of the widow's son (Fig. 14). So well known was Elijah's visit to Sarepta in Phoenicia that the writer of the Gospel of Luke made use of it to support the saying of Jesus that "no prophet is acceptable in his own country," with the historical analogy, "there were many widows in Israel in the days of Elijah . . . and Elijah was sent to none of them, only to Sarepta, in the land of Sidon, to a woman who was a widow" (4:24-26). Thus a popular story from the Old Testament was given a new prominence by the reference to it in Christian writings. It is no wonder that pilgrims on their way to the Holy Land stopped at Sarepta to perform an act of devotion.

Among the scores of pilgrims who have left a written account of their visit to Sarepta only a few took the pains to record observations about the city. Yet those who did record more than the feelings which the holy place evoked have provided us with some clues to the city's history.

As early as the end of the fourth century there was a tower (*turricula*) at Sarepta, presumably to mark for pilgrims the site of the "upper chamber," of Elijah. Paula, a wealthy matron, had embarked from Rome in A.D. 382. After passing through Cyprus and visiting Antioch she made her way south. Her friend and mentor Jerome of Bethlehem wrote of the lady's pilgrimage some years later: "Leaving Berytus, a Roman colony, and the ancient city of Sidon; on the shore of Sarepta, she entered the tower of Helias, in which she adored the Lord and Saviour; she then passed over the sands of Tyre, in which Paul impressed his knees."[1]

A little more than a century was to pass before there was to be another recorded visit. About the year 530 an otherwise unknown Theodosius recorded that there was a church of St. Elijah at Sarepta, a city which impressed the visitor by its size. He recalled correctly that in the Bible "it was called Sarepta of Sidonia, because at that time Sidon was a metropolis to Sarepta," and adds the remark of some importance, "but now Sarepta is the metropolis."[2]

But only a generation after Theodosius had been im-

[1] *The Pilgrimage of the Holy Paula*, in the Publications of the Palestine Pilgrims' Text Society, (hereafter: PPTS), 1, p. 4.

[2] *On the Topography of the Holy Land*, PPTS, 2, p. 16, par. 73.

pressed by the great size of the city, Antoninus Martyr of Placentia described it as "small," but hastened to add that it was "a very Christian city."[3] The visitor had little need of his imagination to recall the memorable deeds of the Hebrew prophet. Antoninus reported that he was shown "the chamber which was built for Helias, and the bed on which he lay, and a marble trough in which the widow (in Scripture) made her bread."

Following hard upon the individual pilgrims were the Crusaders. Toward the end of the twelfth century William of Tyre described the route the Crusaders took as they marched from Sidon to Tyre in the preceding century. Inadvertently he provides an important clue for the location of the city at the time. In describing the route southward he remarks that "they passed on the right the ancient city Sarepta of the Sidonians, the nurse of Elijah, the man of God."[4] Obviously the new site of the village (Sarafand) has not been established, since that would have been as it is today on the left of the coastal road (Fig. 15).

It is a disappointing legacy of observations that we have from the times of the Crusades. No less than 13 travelers from the twelfth through the fourteenth centuries wrote something about Sarepta. The remarks have to do with

such matters as how many miles the city was from Sidon or Tyre—a reminder that travel was arduous—the mention of a beautiful castle or fortress and, of course, a chapel. The latter is said to have been located at the south gate of the city by two travelers, Burchard of Mt. Zion,[5] who wrote at the end of the thirteenth century, and Marino Sanuto,[6] at the beginning of the fourteenth. But for the most part the diaries are otherwise unenlightening.

There is one exception however. Burchard of Mt. Zion was impressed by the ruinous state of Sarepta in 1280: only eight houses were standing, he counted. The metropolis which had so impressed Theodosius on his visit there seven centuries before had almost completely fallen into ruins.

One may properly ask whether the site of this Phoenician city of the Iron Age would have lost its identification with the past had it not been for the strong tradition which attracted so many pious pilgrims. Be that as it may, the itineraries, diaries, and memoirs of visitors from abroad have survived to record the city's fortunes through a long stretch of time which otherwise could have been its dark ages.

Sarepta makes its first appearance in the political history

3 *Of the Holy Places Visited by Antoninus Martyr*, PPTS, 2, p. 3.
4 *A History of Deeds Done Beyond the Sea by William, Archbishop of Tyre*, tr., E. A. Babcock and A. C. Krey, 1943; 1, p. 331; 2, p. 68.
5 *A Description of the Holy Land*, PPTS, 12, p. 13;
6 *Secrets for True Crusaders to Help Them to Recover the Holy Land*, PPTS, 12, p. 25.

15. Nineteenth-century engraving of the village of Sarafand, by W. H. Bartlett

of the Near East in a boastful annal of Sennacherib. The Assyrian king chronicled his triumphal march southward along the Phoenician coast in the year 701 B.C. According to the cuneiform text of a clay prism, now a prize possession of the Oriental Institute of the University of Chicago, the conqueror found little resistance from Sidon and seven satellite cities, of which Sarepta was one.[7]

Luli, king of the Sidonian league, was so frightened by the Assyrian might—or so Sennacherib boasted—that he fled overseas and perished, leaving all "his fortress cities, walled (and well) provided with feed and water for his garrisons."

Apparently the Sidonian cities capitulated without resistance and accepted Sennacherib's puppet, Ethbaal, as king. Tribute was imposed on the newly chosen ruler to be paid to Assyria annually, "without interruption." Thus Sennacherib was able to proceed without losses to Jerusalem and other Palestinian cities in the south, where, in contrast to Phoenicia, battle lines were drawn up and his enemies "sharpened their weapons."

We would like to know why the Sidonian kingdom, of which Sarepta was then a part, surrendered so easily. Was it, as Sennacherib alleged, merely overwhelmed by "the terror-inspiring glamor of my lordship"? Or, did the shrewd

[7] The "Taylor Prism" of Sennacherib is translated by A. Leo Oppenheim in *ANET*[3], pp. 287-88.

Sidonians calculate that the annual tribute demanded for "peace" would be less of a price than losses from a pitched battle?

There is no clear answer; only the possibility that in this accommodation to the realities of military aggression, we may have a clue to a basic Phoenician trait. Traders that they were, the Phoenicians possessed a sense of working compromise that served them well in bargaining. From the historical record of Sarepta as well as from the soundings which we have made at the site, the Phoenicians there managed to survive over many centuries without a major destruction. The record of the other Phoenician cities is also generally that of a peaceful existence.

Although Sennacherib may have felt confident that he had stabilized the Sidonian kingdom by placing Ethbaal on the throne, the arrangement was not to last through the next generation. Esarhaddon, Sennacherib's son, was forced to make a new alignment of the Sidonian city states some twenty years later. "Sarepta," his annals read, "I turned over to (counted into the hand of) Baal (King of Tyre)."[8] Sarepta must have learned that, once having submitted to the Assyrian superpower, other demands were to follow.

Esarhaddon left the Phoenician coast, but not until he had made a treaty with Baal, King of Tyre. From the

[8] R. Borger, *Die Inschriften Asarhaddons, Königs von Assyrien, Archiv für Orientforschung,* Beiheft 9, 1956, 49:16.

fragmentary copy of this treaty preserved on clay, we learn that the Assyrian overlord considered the cargo aboard the ships of King Baal as his own.[9] The treaty stipulates: "If a ship of Baal or of the people of Tyre is ship-wrecked off (the coast of) the land of the Philistines or anywhere on the borders of Assyrian territory, everything that is on the ship belongs to Esarhaddon. ..." Apparently, once again the Phoenician city states were paying for their "peace" with Assyria.

Appended to the treaty is a curse against a breach of the terms of the contract: "May Melqart and Eshmun deliver your land to destruction, your people to be deported. ... May they make disappear food for your mouth, clothes for your body, oil for your ointment." The names of both these gods, Melqart and Eshmun, are found in inscriptions that we were to discover in the ruins at Sarepta (see pp. 98, 102).

For a half dozen centuries after the mention by Esarhaddon of the transfer of Sarepta from the hegemony of Sidon to that of Tyre, the written sources for the fortunes of the city are scanty. In the fourth century Pseudo-Scylax bears witness that Sarepta was then a city of Tyre;[10] and Lycophron, a third century Greek poet, presents us with an obscure mythological reference to Cretans carrying off captive the Sareptan heifer in a bull-formed vessel.[11]

We know little—except what we have learned from the excavations—about the religion of the city before it became Christian and the churches dedicated to Elijah were built. Surely, like that of Sidon and Tyre, its more prominent neighbors, the religion of Sarepta was Phoenician, that is, basically Canaanite in its pattern. The one exception to this almost total dearth of clues for the cult is the tantalizing mention of "the holy god of Sarepta."

"The holy god of Sarepta" appears in three Greek inscriptions, one discovered in southern Italy and the other two from the Phoenician homeland. In 1901 there were found at Puteoli (modern Pozzuoli, near Naples) two fragments of a marble slab with a text which says that in A.D. 79 "... there sailed from Tyre to Puteoli the holy god of Sarepta, conducted by a man of the Elim, in accordance with the divine command."[12] The date is explicit in the Greek text, calculated as May 29, and is probably the date of the landing at Puteoli rather than the date of sailing. A further line in Latin mentioning Domitian, who did not

[9] The Esarhaddon treaty is translated by Erica Reiner in ANET[3], pp. 533-34.

[10] C. Müller, Geographi Graeci minores, 1855-1861, 1, p. 78.

[11] Callimachus, Hymns and Epigrams; Lycophron ..., tr. A. W. Mair, Loeb edition, 1960, lines 1296-1300.

[12] C. C. Torrey published the Yale plaque and a rereading of the Puteoli inscription in "The Exiled God of Sarepta," Berytus, 9, 1948-49, pp. 45-49.

come to power until the fall of A.D. 81, suggests that the memorial had not been erected until some time after the celebrated arrival. Apparently it was a priest—"Elim" is Semitic for gods—who was the custodian of the image during its westward journey.

Some years after the discovery of the Puteoli inscription C. C. Torrey, an American scholar, found in the Yale Babylonian Collection another mention of the Sareptan god, this time on a bronze tablet with three holes by which it had been mounted. The five-line Greek text read: "To the holy god of Sarepta, a fellow-exile has set up this votive offering." Since the provenience of the plaque was said by the dealer who sold it to Yale to have been Syria, Torrey conjectured that in this text there was "a voice from the other end—the beginning—of the voyage of the Phoenician party through the Mediterranean." On their departure some exiles from Sarepta set up a votive offering to their god before setting sail with the divine image.

Yet a third occurrence of this anonymous deity, "the holy god of Sarepta," is upon a stone discovered at Sarafand (Fig. 16).[13] In 1969, a villager reported to Brahim Kawkabani, Inspector of Antiquities for South Lebanon, the finding of a marble block with an inscription. When M. Kawkabani took us to see the inscribed stone it was in a house along the main Sidon-Tyre highway, covered with

[13] Bulletin du Musée de Beyrouth, 24, 1971, pp. 54-56.

16. Inscription with dedication to "the holy god of Sarepta," discovered at Sarafand in 1969

a blanket under a bed. Even in the poorly lit room, we could make out one word in clear Greek letters: CAPAΠΤHN (Sarepta).

Later the Service des Antiquités purchased the marble block from the villager who had discovered it, and they deposited it in the National Museum in Beirut. We were permitted to photograph it and eventually, through the courtesy of the Director, allowed to study and publish it. It appears to be a part of a dedicatory inscription in three lines which had been carved on a step, possibly to an altar. The top line reads "To the holy god of Sarepta," and on the second line are the words "steps along with. . . ." One may surmise that the name of the god of the city was so well known that there was no need to spell it out.

It was not until the seventeenth century that a new kind of visitor made his appearance. His interests ranged over such things as the quality of wine produced at Sarepta, the natural beauty of the area, tombs and ancient remains, and other matters which had been largely ignored by the pilgrims.

Such a visitor to Sarepta was George Sandys, who had reacted against the narrowness of interest on the part of those who had gone before him to the holy places.[14] His aim, he declared, was "to deliver the reader from many errering reports of the too credulous devotee, and too, too vain-glorious."

Traveling in company with "diverse English merchants," he came upon Sarepta on April 25, 1611. In his account he noted the mosque, which was said to have been erected over the widow's house, and then quoted the lines of Sidonius Apollinaris about the wines of Sarepta: "Gazetic, Chian, nor Falernian wine have I: drink then of the

Sareptan vine." The new town of Sarapanta, high on the hill, he described as "hand-some," that is, "moderately large" if he was using the word in a sense now rare.

Proceeding on his way southward, he spotted caves, which were probably the tombs of the Roman period which one sees today at Adloun, and he ventured an opinion as to their function and date. They were "the habitations, as I suppose, of men of the Golden Age, and before the Foundation of Cities." The period of archaeological interest had arrived, even long before the method of dating the ruins had been devised.

Half a century later the Chevalier d'Arvieux paid Sarafand a leisurely visit.[15] In addition to the dominant legend, kept alive now by a beautiful mosque on the sacred spot, he was impressed by the view from the village high on the spur of the mountain, and by its fountain, its olive and fruit trees. To these observations he added what might be called an anthropological note: "There is a dervish who lives in that mosque, who offers fresh water to those who pass and receives whatever alms one wishes to give him."

Richard Pococke, an English divine who was later to become Bishop of Meath, came to Sarafand on May 29,

---

[14] George Sandys, *Sandys Travells, Containing an History of the Original and Present State of the Turkish Empire*, 1670, Book 3, p. 166.

[15] Jean-Baptiste Ladat, *Mémoires du Chevalier d'Arvieux . . . .*, 2, 1735, p. 4.

1738.[16] He was quick to observe that the village on the hill, while bearing a corruption of the ancient name Sarepta, was not the ancient site. That, he observed correctly, was beside the sea. Ruins of a "very ancient building" caught his fancy. In it was "a round plinth, which projected about a foot beyond the pillar, and the edges of it were taken off," he wrote, in what could be called the first description of an artifact from the site. Then he appended, in what is now common archaeological procedure, the citation of a parallel to his discovery: "the whole being exactly after the manner of the very ancient architecture, which I saw in upper Egypt." Both the recording and the citing of an analogy elsewhere anticipate the methods of modern archaeology. Without doubt the plinth that Pococke described and partly measured has long since been broken up or reused as building material; this simple entry with the suggestion of Egyptian influence remains the sole testimony to it.

Not until the nineteenth century was there anything like scientific investigation at Sarepta. Two visitors came, both celebrated for outstanding scholarly achievements. The first was Edward Robinson, the biblical geographer.[17] He came to Sarafand after more than two months of arduous travel through Palestine in 1838. The journey had

been full of hardships and Robinson was physically exhausted when he arrived at Sarepta on Monday, June 25. Served Saturday night in Tyre had been an unhappy one. Served Syrian dishes with rusty knives and forks, he was then given "a miserable red wine, the poorest we tasted in the country." After a Sunday of rest in Tyre, spent bathing in the sea and sleeping on the floor of the servants' house, Robinson set out at 6:00 A.M. on the road to Sidon. He complained of being unwell. Five hours later he approached Sarafand, noting the Wely el-Khudr, which is still standing today beside the modern motor road, and the site of ruins on the left, "indicating however in themselves little more than a mere village."

It was the name "Surafend," as he heard it pronounced by villagers, that interested the philologist Robinson most. The method he had employed throughout Palestine for identifying ancient sites was to observe the similarity between the ancient and the modern place names. Again he applied his hypothesis that ancient names persisted. "In the name" he recorded in his diary, "we here have Zarephath of the Old Testament, and Sarepta of the New." But this similarity was not enough. Robinson had combed the existing literature—Josephus, Jerome, Antoninus, Burchard of Mt. Zion, William of Tyre, Sandys,

16 Richard Pococke, A Description of the East and Some other Countries, 1745, 2, pp. 84-85.

17 Edward Robinson, Biblical Researches, 2, pp. 462-76.

and the Chevalier d'Arvieux—for a complete history of the site to trace its name as far back as he could. All these and other references he gives with scrupulous exactitude in his diary.

Although Robinson spent little more than an hour at Sarafand—he recorded carefully the times of arrival and departure—his visit was important not so much for what he observed as for what he brought by way of learning. No visitor before him had known so much about the written history of the site.

The first archaeologist to come was Ernest Renan. He was the first to publish a scientific account of archaeological remains found in the vicinity of Sarafand. The two folio volumes are entitled *Mission de Phénicie*. What was ready at hand on the surface or in tombs he described and reproduced on the plates of his sumptuous volumes published in 1864. His observations about the tombs near the village of Saksakiye—he believed that they constituted the necropolis of Sarepta—and "two beautiful adjoining rooms cut in the rock at the shore of the sea" are of interest. The latter we found very much as described by Renan when we first visited Sarafand in 1968. Alas, they were used for a fortified house for young commando fighters in the fall of 1970; now they have been blasted away along with the concrete which had been laid over them for a roof.

When we began our first season of work at Sarafand in 1969, the items we have listed constituted about all that was known about Sarepta's history.[18] Visitors had come throughout the centuries for a variety of reasons: to survive in a time of famine, collect tribute, set up a new ruler, worship at its holy place, fight in a holy crusade, or describe the antiquities which lay upon the surface. But in this impressive documentation for the continuing life of Sarepta through almost two millennia there was little description of the city and its inhabitants. It was this missing detail that we hoped to recover.

[18] For a more detailed treatment of the reference to Sarepta see my "Sarepta in Tradition and History," John Reumann, ed., *Understanding the Sacred Text*, 1972, pp. 101-14.

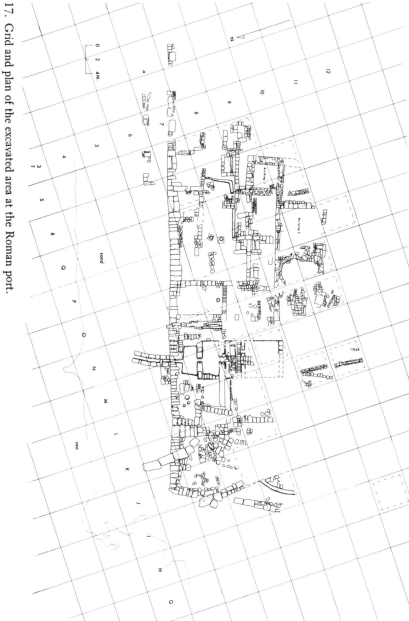

17. Grid and plan of the excavated area at the Roman port.

IV

The Roman Port

THE first season's work produced nothing to indicate that the Phoenicians had ever been at Sarepta. Beside the southwestern harbor at Ras esh-Shiq, where we dug for eight weeks in 1969, not a sherd of evidence was found for occupation before the Roman period. Yet we did discover that sometime in the first century A.D. seafaring successors to the Phoenicians on the Lebanon coast had constructed a quay, a system for provisioning seagoing vessels with drinking water, and warehouses for storing goods received and freight to be shipped. Moreover, during a half dozen centuries these facilities were modified, or enlarged, or added to as the traffic of the port required.

The plan of the walls that had survived at the port was complex (Fig. 17). The foundation for a new building had often been laid with stones robbed from the superstructure of an older one nearby, while the foundation of the older building, and sometimes its floor, had been left intact. The occupation and use of the area had been continuous from the building of the first walls on bedrock until the final abandonment of the site. There had been no general destruction by fire and no periods of desertion.

This sector of the city had been a public area given over to commerce. Not only were the walls built of massive, well-dressed blocks of sandstone but even the debris that covered the ruins indicated public rather than private use of the buildings. This debris contained tesserae from mosaic floors, fragments of marble, ceramic roof tiles, and designs of molded decoration in plaster (Fig. 18). Conspicuously absent were walls of the more modest materials characteristic of domestic architecture. Also absent was equipment—such as ovens, hand mills for grinding grain, and cooking pots—usually found in private houses.

In the first major period in the development of the port a rectangular quay, measuring 12.60 m. in width and at least 14.50 m. in length, had been constructed on a natural promontory so as to be accessible from the sea on three of its sides (Fig. 17, L/N-6/8; Fig. 19). Although the clamps which bound the stones of the quay together had been pried loose by looters, traces of rust in the dovetailed notches provided evidence for the use of iron for the brackets, which had probably been set in lead (Fig. 20). It was clear from small shells imbedded in the in-

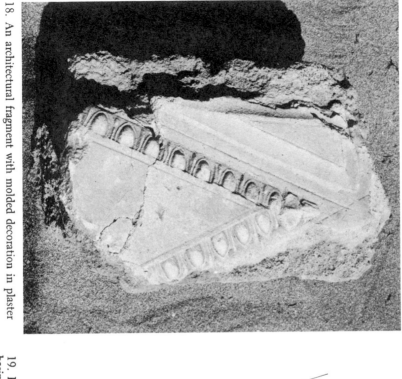

18. An architectural fragment with molded decoration in plaster

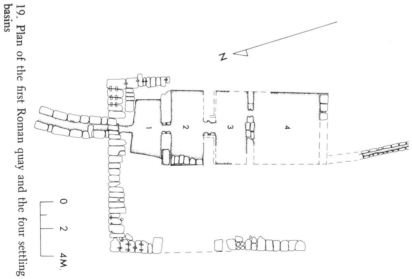

19. Plan of the first Roman quay and the four settling basins

20. Notches for clamp that held stones of the quay

crustation on the face of the walls next to the sea that the sea had actually extended to its base. Yet so well built was the wall directly opposite the sea that not a single stone had been dislodged from its foundation.

The outer faces of the blocks in the quay wall were dressed in a distinctive pattern (Fig. 21). A margin had been drafted around the four edges of the stone so as to leave a boss, or projection, in the center. A similar feature in the masonry of an important building to the east, Building 1 (Fig. 17, Q/R-9/10), suggests that it belongs to the same period of construction as that of the quay.

The first indication we had that the stone structure built on a rocky promontory that extends into the sea was a quay for ships came with the discovery of a mooring-ring (see Fig. 19) set into its east wall and securely locked to it with clamps (Fig. 22). Its location on the east, rather than on the seaward wall, where one would expect it to have been, makes it likely that an estuary had originally extended inward beside the quay. Small ships could have tied up there well protected from the waves.

Mooring-rings had not previously been found at harbors along the eastern coast of the Mediterranean. In the West, however, they have long been known at the Emporium of Rome and at Ostia, where they may be seen within the hexagonal basin in which ships were moored in the time

21. Marginally drafted stones in a wall of Building 1 of the first-century port

22. Mooring-ring built into the quay of the first Roman port

of Trajan.[1] Even at such an unlikely place as on an island lying at the north end of the Dead Sea a mooring-ring has been discovered recently.[2]

The ring set in the Sarepta quay, however, has a puzzling feature. In addition to the hole, 17 cm. in diameter, bored through the block, there is a well-fashioned molding that projects from the underside of the curved ring. There can be no doubt that the design was intentional. Did the projecting ledge have a practical function, such as to make the securing of the line to the ship easier? Or was it merely a decorative detail which served to satisfy the aesthetic sense of a stonecutter working on a construction which otherwise was monotonous? The detail remains a puzzle.

There is a graphic answer to how the mooring-ring was used in Roman times. In the Torlonia Museum in Italy a bas-relief of the late second century pictures a ship tied to a ring of a quay with a heavy line (Fig. 23).[3] A gangway, of what appears to be a single plank, bridges the gap between deck and dock. A stevedore with an amphora on his shoulder, makes his way precariously across the un-

steady passageway. One may suppose that a ship at Sarepta was unloaded in much the same way.

A hint as to the cargo a ship would have carried from the port is provided by an ancient edict on the subject of price-fixing. At the beginning of the fourth century A.D. the Roman Emperor Diocletian published some ceilings on prices, and among the commodities listed are some that are designated as Phoenician: honey, shoots of palm, pine-nuts, and hides.[4] All of these items would have been available in the region of Sarepta.

Besides these products the Edict of Diocletian lists as Phoenician manufactured items which were at the time, apparently, making their way to the Roman markets from the coast of the eastern Mediterranean. Among the items mentioned are: sandals, purple silk, wool, and linen, not only spun but woven and made up into shirts, dalmatics (a loose garment with very wide sleeves), wraps, veils, hoods, and handkerchiefs.

From a half century later, but still well within the period when the Sarepta port was in operation, there is extant an anonymous work with the ambitious title of

[1] For four mooring blocks at the Emporium of Rome, see E. Nash, Pictorial Dictionary of Ancient Rome, 1, 1968, p. 382, fig. 465. They appear within Trajan's hexagonal basin at Ostia (G. Calza, Notizie degli Scavi di Antichità, 1, 1925, p. 56, fig. 1).

[2] Zeitschrift des deutschen Palästina-Vereins, 82, 1966, pp. 139-48.
[3] R. Meiggs, Roman Ostia, 1960, pl. 20.
[4] J. P. Brown, The Lebanon and Phoenicia, 1, 1969, pp. 43-47.

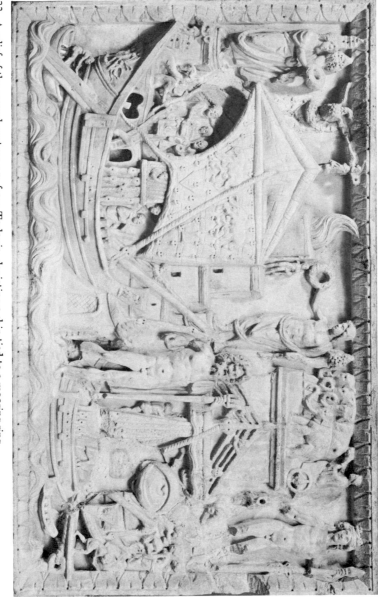

23. A relief of the second century A.D. from Torlonia, depicting a ship tied to a mooring-ring

24. Cleaning the mud from the filtering basin next to the sea

"Description of the Whole World and its Peoples."[5] The coastal cities of Byblos, Tyre, and Beirut are said to have exported linen cloth, and Sarepta specifically is mentioned in connection with the export of genuine purple, as well as the staples of grain, oil, and wine.

We did not find, nor did we expect to find, any trace of the cargo which passed through the port at Sarepta. We did discover, however, that at Sarepta ships could be provisioned with drinking water, an essential for any long journey, like that from Sarepta to Puteoli, for example (cf. p. 43).

Half the area of the quay we have described was occupied by rock-cut basins. The first to be discovered was a tank, 2 by 4.25 m., hewn from the rock, directly behind the north well of the quay (Fig. 19.1). As workmen cleaned it they first encountered moist soil, then mud (Fig. 24). As they went deeper the workmen had to dip out the debris with buckets as they stood knee-deep in the slush. Pottery and other artifacts had to be virtually strained out. Finally at the end of a working day they reached the rock bottom, which was but .28 m. below the present level of the sea.

By the next morning the basin was again half filled with water and the Sisyphean task had to be repeated. It was not clear at the time whether the water had seeped in

from crevices in the rock floor or had flowed in through a passageway which led to the sea. The narrow opening between the basin and the sea had vertical notches cut at each side, obviously slots into which a sluice gate had been seated (Fig. 25.) By raising or removing the barrier the basin could have been emptied through a stone channel or culvert that extended for about 5 m. seaward.

25. Cuttings in the rock which provided a seat for a sluice gate between two basins

In the south wall of the basin there appeared another opening opposite to that in the wall on the sea side. This opening, too, had a similar fitting of grooves cut into the sides for securing a sluice gate. It was not surprising, therefore, to find a second basin (Fig. 19.2) cut from the live rock immediately behind the first. When it, in turn, was completely cleared to the bottom, which was approximately at the same level of the first, there appeared once again a passageway with its gate opening southward. Behind the second basin was yet a third (Fig. 19.3) and it too had a passageway with its gate leading to the fourth element of the construction, a large tank approximately twice the size of Basin 3.

There remained no trace of the gates which had been secured by the vertical grooves in the walls of the passageways between the interconnected basins. However, during the excavation of the submerged channel complex at Kenchreai, the eastern port of ancient Corinth, Joseph W. Shaw did find sections of gates *in situ* within grooves cut in the passageways between a series of basins.[6] Both stone slabs and wooden boards had been used. It is reasonable to assume that either or both materials had been used at Sarepta as removable barriers.

Altogether there were four rectangular basins cut into the rock on which the quay had been built, connected by three gates to control the flow of water from one to the other and equipped with a fourth gate to the sea. From the orientation of the plan for the quay it was evident that the system of contiguous basins had either been constructed as an integral part of the port or that the port had been built to incorporate the water system within it. The quay and the tanks belonged together.

6 *American Journal of Archaeology*, 71, 1967, p. 225.

26. Three steps leading from the wharf into the dipping basin for filling amphorae with fresh water

The function of the basins was not as evident as their plan. Could they have been fish tanks, which are described in such detail by Columella (see p. 65)? But these had channels to provide a constant circulation of sea water; ours did not. Unless the level of the Mediterranean had changed in two thousand years—a possibility of course—the sea could not have filled the basins, the bottoms of which were at approximately the same level as the sea at high tide. There was a possibility that these puzzling containers could have served the dye industry, for which Sarepta and other cities on the coast had been famous. But there were no dye stains on the walls, no discarded *murex* shells.

Eventually, some decisive pieces of evidence appeared. In cleaning the surface of the north side of the quay we encountered three steps leading down to a small tank, .60 by .80 m, which had been hewn from the live rock (Fig. 26). A hole in the wall that separated it from Basin 1 would have allowed water to fill it. When the remains of four amphorae were found crushed on the lowest of the three steps we were persuaded that the small tank was indeed a dipping basin from which sailors who called at the port filled their amphorae with drinking water.

With the discovery of this feature the entire picture came into focus. The four connected basins had been constructed to remove the sediment from surface water and make it potable. A section of the conduit which had brought the water from the hills to the first basin (Fig. 19.4) indicated that the system held fresh and not sea water (Fig. 27). In Basin 4 some of the sediment sank to the bottom, as the clearer liquid passed over the top of the sluice gate to the next basin, where further settling took place. After three such treatments the water collected in the basin beside the quay, available to ships. Periodically the sluice gates could be removed and the entire system flushed of its muddy sediment; the process could then be started over again. A simple device, but useful.

It was difficult to determine precisely the date for the construction of the water system. There were diagonal striations from the tools with which the basins had been cut from the live rock, but as yet there is not enough evidence for the kinds of tools used in the Roman period to make use of the marks they left for dating. The filling within the basins could have been laid down several centuries after the time of construction and first use. And, if our theory about the periodical cleaning of the sediment is correct, most of the residue from the early periods of use would long since have been flushed out to sea.

There was a clue, however, for the latest possible date for the construction. In the bottom of the seaward basin a particularly keen-eyed workman spotted a badly corroded bronze coin within the mud. When it was cleaned

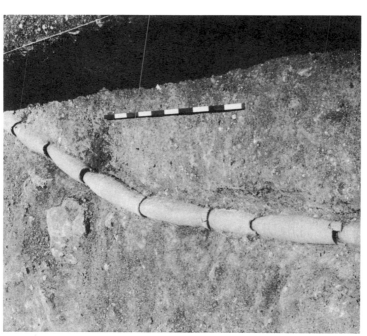

by electrolysis in a solution of sodium hydroxide with zinc pellets, the head of Melqart was visible on the obverse and a Greek inscription appeared on the reverse. It had been minted at Tyre in A.D. 112-113.[7]

Since the coin obviously had been dropped during the time the system was functioning or at least before the basin was filled in, the date of its construction must have been earlier. How much we cannot say. Other coins found about the site suggest a first century A.D. date for the initial use of the quay. The earliest precisely dated coin among the 98 identifiable coins discovered at the site was minted in A.D. 93-94.[8] Since it was found in the vicinity of Building 1, built of drafted masonry like that of the quay and set directly on the bedrock, a reasonable date for the earliest use of the area as a port is toward the end of the first century A.D.

The remains of two other constructions belong to the early port facility (Buildings 1 and 2 in Fig. 17). Both are built of ashlar blocks that show no previous use and their foundations are set firmly on the bedrock. While only three of the four sides of Building 1 remain, the care with which its north wall was constructed attests its im-

[7] G. F. Hill, *Catalogue of the Greek Coins of Phoenicia*, 1910, p. 267, no. 356.
[8] D. Baramki, *The Coins Exhibited in the Archaeological Museum of the American University of Beirut*, 1968, no. 100.

27. Section of the conduit leading from the hills to the filtering system

28. The enlarged quay, extending more than 44 m. along the shore

29. Mooring-ring of the enlarged quay, with grooves scored by lines from ships

portance. The stones of the north wall, 1 m. wide, are marginally dressed and those of the lower course are meticulously fitted to the contours of the bedrock on which they rest (Fig. 21). Building 2, situated to the southwest of Building 1, is considerably larger. Its north wall, preserved for a distance of 10.90 m., was built in the header-and-stretcher construction and coated with a layer of hard plaster, which extended downward over a sloping abutment to the bedrock. Obviously this coating served the purpose of keeping water away from the foundation. Within the rectangular outline of the structure there appears an elliptical structure as yet unexplained. It was bonded to the stones of the north wall of the surrounding building. It seems reasonably certain that both of these monumental buildings were contemporaneous with the rectangular quay.

Eventually the modest first-century quay proved inadequate and the seaward wall was extended in a straight line to the east and to the west for a total length of more than 44 m. (Fig. 28). How much farther the new wharf ran to the east it was impossible to determine since that end had been destroyed either by stone looters or the action of the sea, or both. The builders of the enlargement had made use of massive ashlar blocks, many of them with cuttings that evidenced previous use in monumental buildings.

When the earlier quay was enlarged it had been necessary to fill in the estuary that extended beside the mooring-ring. With this device no longer accessible from the sea, a new ring was built into the extended quay (Fig. 29). It was similar in design to the earlier stone—the puzzling ledge on the under side had been duplicated—but the hole was larger and displayed evidence of considerable use. On the edges of the opening well-worn grooves had been cut as the tide and wind had tightened and slackened the lines that bound the ships to land.

Along the eastern extension of the quay a series of rectangular rooms had been constructed of large stone blocks obviously robbed from other buildings. The largest and best preserved of the rooms measured 4 by 6.50 m. Although the floors of the rooms had generally been robbed, one pavement of stones did remain intact (Fig. 30). It would seem reasonable to interpret the remains of these rooms beside the quay as warehouses.

When did the enlargement of the port take place? One indicator for the date points to the beginning of the Byzantine period in the fourth century. Throughout the area of the excavation there were recovered 98 coins that could be identified with known mints. Every century from the first to the eleventh was represented, with the one exception of the ninth. The first three centuries were documented by only six percent of the total; but coins minted in the fourth century constituted 49 percent of all the coins found. If we assume that sailors and traders at the port were no more careful of their money in one century than in another, then the fourth century must have seen a burgeoning of commercial activity. The enlarged quay may well have provided facilities for the spurt in trade indicated by the increase in lost coins.

After the discovery of the quay and installations associated with it, we proceeded to map the semicircular harbor and to record the depths of water at regular intervals (Fig. 31).

It was immediately clear why the waves from heavy seas would break about 100 m. offshore and then be dissipated into foamy ripples. An L-shaped natural reef, 1 m. below the surface, acts as a natural mole to provide shelter from the open sea (Fig. 31). At each end of the reef there are channels, 3 m. deep, which would allow access for ships to the harbor and also make possible the circulation of water, an aid for keeping the harbor from silting up.

Another feature in the region of the natural harbor was man-made. It was a tank, 3.10 m. square, cut from the live rock of a promontory that reaches out a few meters into the sea at the west end of the quay (Figs. 32 and 33). Erosion had taken its toll of the seaward side of the basin, but the original plan and dimensions were clearly discernible.

30. Paved floor of a warehouse beside the quay

31. Plan of the harbor

QUAY

100 M.

50

0

32. Fish tank cut from the rock of the promontory at Ras esh-Shiq

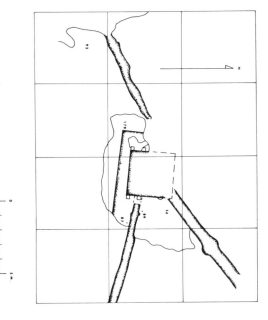

33. Plan of the fish tank with the channels to the sea

The bottom of the tank is slightly below the level of the sea, and at the top there appear notches on two sides, which could have served to secure beams that supported a covering. There are three openings in the walls of the tank; originally there had been four, one for each corner. These apertures led into channels which had been cut into the rock of the promontory for a distance of about 8 m, until they reached the sea. At low tide the canals were empty, but with the rising tide they were filled and carried sea water inward, providing a circulation of water within the confines of the basin. Twice a day the water flowed in and out.

In the first century A.D. Lucius Junius Moderatus Columella wrote a treatise on agriculture, in which he gives directions for constructing a saltwater pool for fish. His advice is as follows:

. . . the best pond is one which is so situated that the incoming tide of the sea expels the water of the previous tide . . . for a pond most resembles the open sea if it is stirred by the winds and its water is constantly renewed. . . . The pond is either hewn in the rock, which only rarely occurs, or built of plaster on the shore. . . . If the nature of the ground permits, channels should be provided for the water on every side of the fish-pond. . . . It will be well to remember that gratings made of brass with small holes should be fixed in front of the channels through which the fish-pond pours out its waters, to prevent the fish from escaping.[9]

This description fits the tank at Sarepta so well that there can be little doubt as to the use to which it was put. One other remark Columella made is of particular interest when considering the function of this particular example. It is that fishponds are also used for growing "purple-producing shell-fish."[10] It is not impossible that the tank had the more specialized function, that of growing the *murex*, the source of the purple dye for which Sarepta was famous in Roman times.

Ours is not the first example of a Roman fish tank which has come to light. At the harbor of Chersonisos, on the north coast of Crete, three of these tanks with channels leading to the sea were discovered by John Leatham and Sinclair Hood. Two more were found at Mochlos, also on the north coast, and in one of them was a fragment of stone grill, which is believed by the excavators to have been a filter that permitted the flow of water in and out while preventing the fish from escaping.

Two additional buildings within the port area provide

8. 17,

9 *Lucius Junius Moderatus Columella on Agriculture*, translated by E. S. Forster and E. H. Heffner, Loeb edition, 1954,

10 *Columella* 8. 16. 7.

34. The furnace of a Roman bath in the port area

35. Foundation of a Byzantine church to the southwest of the quay

us with information about activities at Sarepta, during the Byzantine period. The first was a bath, which had been built only 15 m. back of the quay (Fig. 34). A caldarium, a steaming room with a pool of hot water, must have been particularly welcome to a sailor who had spent days cramped abroad his small craft.

The upper part of the bath had long since been destroyed. What remained was the praefurnium, the furnace for heating the water. Pillars of square and round clay disks that had once supported the floor of the bath stood to a height of *ca.* 35 cm. among the ash of the last use. The lines of an earlier building had been utilized as foundations for the hypocaust, the heating system.

It would have been surprising had we found no remains of a church in an area occupied in the Roman and Byzantine periods when Christians kept alive the tradition of Elijah's visit to Sarepta. The foundation of a church did appear at the southwest corner of the field we had rented for exploration (Fig. 35). While making a sounding 5 m. square, some 90 m. to the southwest of the west end of the quay, there emerged the foundation to a building consisting of six courses of chalk set firmly on bedrock. Nine of the stones were painted with red Greek letters—H and Θ—the quarrier's mark for identifying either the source or the position for which the stones were intended. All the superstructure had disappeared, with the exception of a

36. Marble base of a column from the church

37. Greek letter incised on the underside of the column base

marble base for a column (Fig. 36), on the underside of which was incised the Greek letter Φ within a circular field (Fig. 37).

The plan of what remains of the foundation of the building consists of a corner at which two curved walls meet. If the arcs of these walls are projected to semicircles, as they have been in a reconstruction of the plan in Fig. 38, there appears half of the plan of the familiar tetraconch church of Byzantine architecture. If this symmetrical plan is completed by the addition of the opposite conchs, the reconstruction of the church measures approximately 17.5 by 19.5 m.[11]

What we have learned about Sarepta in the Roman and Byzantine periods comes from a limited sounding within what must have been a vast area of occupation. There is no evidence for any settlement beside this harbor before the first century A.D. Following the building of the earlier quay with its water system, there were, to judge from the frequency of datable coins, two major periods of development. In the fourth century there was a surge of building. The quay was greatly expanded, warehouses were built. This was done mostly with massive ashlar blocks salvaged from buildings that had fallen into ruins

[11] A triconch church was discovered in Bethany in 1881 (16.20 x 19.44 m. overall), *Oriens Christianus*, Ser. 3, 5, 1930, p. 237.

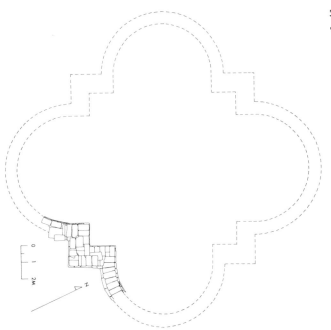

38. Reconstructed plan of the Byzantine church

in other parts of the city. The second largest number of coins, about one-third of the total, belongs to the sixth century, the period to which we would date the latest buildings on the site. Tentatively we would place the church, and possibly the hypocaust within the same century. After that, datable coins were scarce: only seven come from the seventh century, three from the eighth, and one each from the tenth and eleventh. Thus it appears that after the seventh century the site beside the harbor was virtually deserted, visited only occasionally.

After a season of excavations at the site of the Roman and Byzantine port we had succeeded in documenting about six centuries of Sarepta's history. To be sure the general cultures of this period are well known; but we had at least augmented the history of this coastal site and discovered some details which were unique. There remained yet another area where we might hope to find remains of the Phoenician period, and we decided to move there for a trial sounding.

V

The Phoenician Settlement

THE site picked at the start of the second season as a place to begin another search for Phoenician remains was the mound at Ras el-Qantara, some 500 m. to the northeast of the Roman harbor. It is the highest point on the shoreline at Sarafand, rising abruptly from the sea to a height of 12 m. There was the possibility, we reckoned, that this small hill was not a natural formation but the accumulation of debris from centuries of human occupation. The protected bay immediately to the north of the promontory on which the mound stood would have provided a convenient harbor. This could have been the Phoenician settlement.

The western face of the promontory had been eroded by heavy seas. In the scarp, stubs of walls and masses of Roman sherds could be seen, but nothing earlier. Scouring the surface of the fields on top of the mound for diagnostic sherds that might date its occupation, we found two handles from amphorae that had been imported from the Hellenistic Island of Rhodes. They could be dated to the Hellenistic period by the labels in Greek which had been stamped on them. Obviously the site had been occupied at least

two centuries before the Roman port was built. Below the Hellenistic debris there might be the remains of an Iron Age settlement, but on the surface there was no evidence —not a single potsherd—to witness a Phoenician presence.

The particular field chosen for sounding was an irregularly shaped plot of about two acres (Plot 132 in Fig. 39) belonging to Mohammed Kawtarani, who had planted it with wheat some two months earlier. Negotiations for rental were amicable but prolonged since it was difficult to explain why we could not wait until the wheat was harvested. After two weeks our impatience prevailed and a contract for a three-year lease of the property was signed.

A grid with coordinates running east-west and north-south was staked out, each 5 m. square was given a letter-number designation to serve in recording the locus of finds, and the new site was called Area II. Within this large area—the grid comprised 252 squares—we selected two locations, each measuring 10 by 10 m., for testing the stratification. The first, which was labeled Sounding X

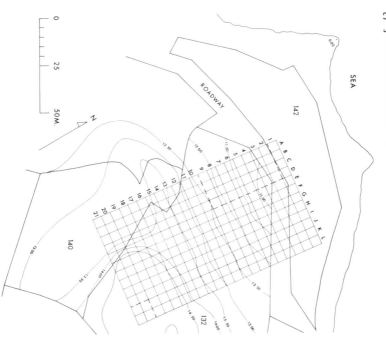

39. Contour map and grid plan for Area II, with excavated areas indicated by dotted line

(squares C/D-6/7 in Fig. 39), lies close to the harbor which is used today as a port for village fishermen: settlement beside such a protected anchorage would have been likely throughout every period of the city's history and particularly in the centuries when the Phoenicians had engaged in maritime commerce. The second area, Sounding Y (K/L-20/21 in Fig. 39), lies on the highest part of the mound: such an eminence, we judged, would have provided the most valuable sites for important or public buildings. Since there was no evidence on the surface for ancient occupation except for broken pottery, we were forced to resort to such general assumptions in making a decision as to where to begin excavation.

Probes into each of these two plots disclosed buildings and artifacts which matched in date those that had been found in the lower levels at the Roman port: the Roman city had evidently been extensive. Below the Roman levels there were buildings which could be assigned to the Hellenistic period by coins of Seleucid mint and pottery which has long been known to be characteristic of the period.

The first evidence that there had been a settlement at Sarafand prior to the Hellenistic period consisted of two pieces of burnished red-slip ware uncovered in Sounding X on the morning of April 27, 1970 (Fig. 40). One had belonged to a high-footed stand (possibly a support

THE PHOENICIAN SETTLEMENT

[73]

40. The first two pieces of burnished red-slip ware to appear in Sounding X

for an incense bowl) and the other, to a large krater with a two-loop horizontal handle; both exhibited a finish which has long been recognized as a characteristic feature of the ceramic repertoire of the Phoenicians both in their homeland and abroad.

The red color and the smooth, polished surface are the products of a distinctive technology. After the potter had fashioned a vessel from plastic clay and allowed it to dry to a leather hardness, he coated it with a creamlike solution of finer clay which had a high iron content. Fired in a kiln, this coating produced a red surface that enhanced considerably the appearance of an otherwise drab and coarse vessel. An additional step was eventually introduced in this process of fabrication to make the vessel even more pleasing aesthetically, and, at the same time, impervious to liquids. After the slip had been applied, the surface was polished with a pebble or other smooth object so that the pores of the vessel were sealed. When it emerged from the kiln its red surface glistened and looked, in fact, more like bronze than the cheaper ceramic product that it was. The production of burnished red-slip ware was dependent upon the availability of a clay that would produce the red color and the skill of a potter who knew how to apply and fire it properly.

The diffusion of this particular technique from the Phoenician homeland, where it seems to have been de-veloped, to sites in the Western Mediterranean provides evidence for the history of Phoenician colonization. At Carthage, for example, Pierre Cintas noted that red-slip ware appeared only in the level of the very earliest settlement,[1] in the later levels of occupation it ceased to be

[1] *Manuel d'archéologie punique*, 1, 1970, pp. 375-82.

found. Thus, he concluded that red-slip ware was imported, never made locally. Either the potters who worked at Carthage did not know how to produce the shiny, red finish on the surface of pots, or they lacked the proper clays for making it.

Red-slip ware has been recognized at other colonial sites. In southern Spain this *cerámica de barniz rojo* has appeared on and near the coast, where it displaced the older local ceramic traditions.[2] Examples of it had been found not only at numerous sites within the Mediterranean basin, but even beyond Gibraltar at Mogador, a Phoenician colony on the Atlantic coast of Morocco.[3]

The first glimpse of the two sherds of red-slip were in Sounding X, exhibiting as they did a hallmark of Phoenician culture, was not a mirage. In the same deposit red-slip ware was found in profusion; the new forms of rims, bases, handles from jars, and saucer lamps could not be recorded according to the type series which had been painstakingly worked out for classifying the Roman and Hellenistic forms. The ceramic material was strikingly different in form as well as in finish.

Within the five baskets of pottery which were collected on the first day of the discovery of this new level there was not a single whole vessel, only sherds from pots which no longer served the purpose for which they had been

formed and fired. Yet these broken pieces from a waste heap constituted the first collection of Iron Age forms to have been discovered at a stratified Phoenician site on the coast of Lebanon.

As excavations were continued in the two areas which had been selected to test the stratigraphy, it became apparent that there was an essential difference between the uses to which each area had been put. Sounding X had been an industrial sector, where dye was extracted from the *murex*, olives were crushed and pressed for their oil, and pottery was manufactured. Industrial use of the area had frequently destroyed the sequence of deposits of occupational debris. It was the potter who had done the most damage to the stratification. In digging a pit for the firing chamber of a kiln or in excavating a basin for washing clay, he had cut through earlier accumulations. Instead of carting away the debris from his excavations, filled as it was with artifacts of earlier centuries, he merely spread it around the pottery-making area to make a new floor slightly higher than the one below. Thus, the reconstruction of the original sequence of layered artifacts is often problematical and sometimes virtually impossible in Sounding X.

There was less disturbance in Sounding Y (Fig. 41). Only two kilns and a few pits had disturbed this area, where people had lived simply in modest homes. When a

2 E. Cuadrado, in *Tartessos*, V *Symposium*, 1969, pp. 257-90.
3 A. Jodin, *Mogador comptoir phénicien du Maroc atlantique, Etudes et travaux d'archéologie marocaine,* II, 1966, pp. 77-120.

41. Stratum E in Sounding Y, with three of the walls of Room 38 visible

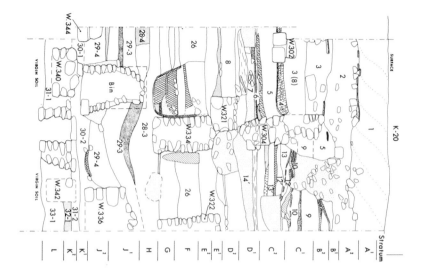

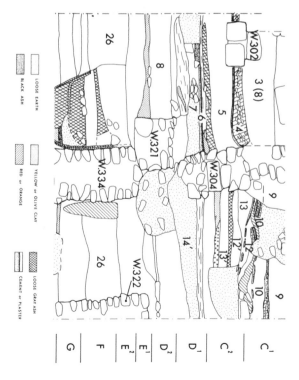

42. Vertical section of the west side of II-K-20, showing layers of debris (labeled with numbers) and walls (numbers preceded by W). Drawn by William P. Anderson

LOOSE EARTH

BLACK ASH

RED or ORANGE

YELLOW or OLIVE CLAY

LOOSE GRAY ASH

CEMENT or PLASTER

through the Hellenistic period, we shall consider only strata G through C, which cover the period extending from the end of the Late Bronze through the Iron Age. A brief synopsis of each of the five strata—we shall refer to them as cities even though the area from which the sample of artifacts come is but a fraction of the city to which it belonged—will serve to illustrate the gradual change in the life style of the inhabitants from period to period.

Stratum G. That the area had once been built over was evident from stubs of some stone walls and the trenches left by looters who had salvaged stones from others, but it was impossible to obtain a complete plan of a house (Fig. 43a). A date of the late thirteenth century B.C. for the stratum is provided by an imported Mycenaean IIIC:1 bowl, decorated with antithetic spirals and a solar disk between them (Fig. 44), a vessel which has close parallels at the site of Enkomi on Cyprus.

The assemblage of locally made pottery displays a wide variety of forms: storage jars—both amphorae (Fig. 45) and large pithoi—bowls, kraters, plates, and cooking pots (Fig. 46). Mixed with the pottery were other artifacts normally found in living areas. For example, a clay plaque that had belonged to a lamp bracket is incised with a geometric design (Fig. 47), a scarab on the face of which appears the Egyptian *wajet* symbol (Fig. 48), a bronze ear-

house replaced an older one, a shallow trench was dug for laying a new foundation and stones were salvaged from the older superstructure, yet the disturbance was minimal. It was, therefore, in this predominantly residential quarter that the floors of successive houses built up in layers that preserved intact the record of changing styles and technological development through the long history of the site.

Altogether, 11 strata of occupation, each with its own distinctive building plan, were recognized within the 8.10 m. of accumulated debris found in Sounding Y; in seven of these strata two phases of use could be detected, either by the appearance of minor structural changes in buildings or by the appearance of a new floor on top of an older one. The complexity of the problem of identifying each of these strata is apparent in the drawing of the vertical section of the west side of plot II-K-20 (Fig. 42). Debris from human occupation often accumulated at a greater rate in one place than in another; floors were frequently nothing more than tightly packed earth; artificial fills, pits for ash or refuse, bins for storage, trenches for foundations—these are some of the anomalies which must be reckoned with in working out the stratigraphy.

Since our concern here is with the Phoenician levels within the longer sequence, which extends from the first occupation on virgin soil or bedrock at the beginning of the Late Bronze period, at approximately 1600 B.C., down

43a. Plans for Strata G-C in Sounding Y (each 10 m. square)

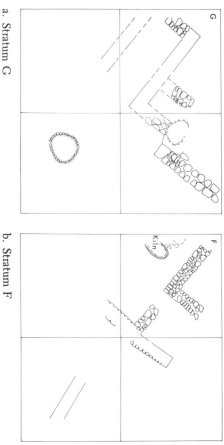

a. Stratum G

b. Stratum F

ring, a cylindrical clay bead, a spindle whorl, and a loom weight.

City G evidenced industrial as well as residential use. Fragments of two crucibles coated with slag and a shapeless piece of metal were found within its debris. Three puzzling basins (two shown in the plan in Fig. 43a) may have been used in the smelting process. The best preserved of the three had been constructed by first digging a pit, 2.40 m. deep and about 1.50 m. in diameter, and then

lining it with field stones. The opening at the top had been partly covered with a flat stone and a platform of cement had been laid over the stone and extended eastward until it met the face of a stone wall. The pit was found to be partly filled with brown earth and charcoal. The lining of loosely set stones suggests that the construction was actually a sump designed to provide underground drainage rather than an ordinary bin for storage.

A possible explanation for its function, as well as for that

c. Stratum E

d. Stratum D

e. Stratum C

of a better-preserved example found in Sounding X, is provided by a similar construction excavated recently at the Cypriot site of Enkomi. There, a cement platform with a drain leading into a sump was a part of a larger metal-lurgical complex.[4] Jacques Lagarce, in his study of the industrial installation at Enkomi, interprets the sloping cement platform as the hard surface on which copper ore was crushed and washed, and the adjacent pit as a device for disposing of the water used in the cleaning process. If

the Sarepta sump tanks served a similar function, other elements of the metal-working complex should appear when the surrounding plots are explored. Until then, the explanation of these features of City G must remain conjectural.

Stratum F. City F was built according to a new plan, but its lines can only partially be filled in. Two large ash-filled courtyards, part of a room with a doorway opening

[4] *Alasia I*, Mission archéologique d'Alasia, 4, 1971, pp. 381-99.

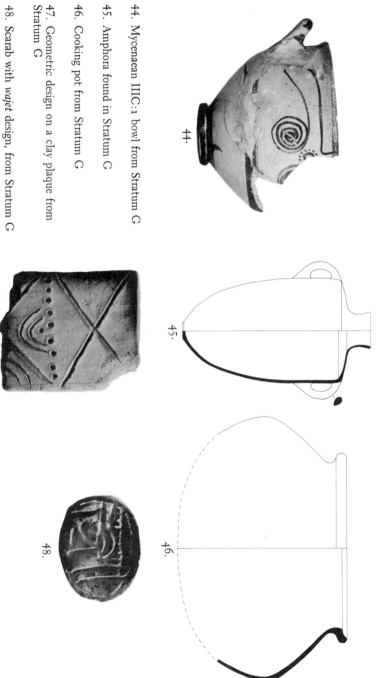

44. Mycenaean IIIC:1 bowl from Stratum G

45. Amphora found in Stratum G

46. Cooking pot from Stratum G

47. Geometric design on a clay plaque from Stratum G

48. Scarab with *wajet* design, from Stratum G

44.

45.

46.

47.

48.

51. Leaded bronze weight in the form of a heifer

into one of the courts, and a potter's kiln can be identified (Fig. 43b). The kiln is a bilobate structure of the same plan used in the industrial area of Sounding X, except that the clay lining for the firing chamber had been plastered directly against the side of the pit that had been dug for it instead of on a stone lining. Imbedded in the ash which had accumulated from the firing of the kiln was a triangular potter's tool, pierced with a hole to provide a convenient grip for the forefinger (Fig. 49).

The ceramic forms of this stratum are in general similar to those found in City G, although the quantity of sherds counted is almost twice that found in the earlier level. A decorated terracotta rattle (Fig. 50) was found in perfect condition; clay pellets inside produced the sounds from this simple musical instrument.

49. Potter's tool fashioned from a potsherd, found in Stratum F

50. Terracotta rattle from Stratum F

52. Stamp seal from Stratum E, with its impression

An impressive product of a craftsman in metal is a weight in the form of a heifer with her legs drawn up under her and tail curled over her back (Fig. 51). When the dirt was cleaned from this object, the greenish blue color of the patina indicated that it had been cast of bronze or copper. Yet, the object was much too heavy to have been made of these metals. Further cleaning revealed cracks on the surface in which the white oxide of lead could be seen. The hollow bovine figure had been filled with lead, as had a similar weight found in Niveau 1 at Ras Shamra, which lies about 250 km. to the north of Sarepta.

Stratum E. The first private dwelling to be found in the area of the sounding was built in City E (Room 38 in Fig. 43C). It is a rectangular room (2.40 m. by 3.80 m.)

equipped with two circular ovens for baking bread; the better preserved of the two was approximately .70 m. in diameter. Yet the area cannot be said to have been exclusively domestic since a potter continued to make use of the kiln built in the previous stratum of occupation. The tradition represented by the pottery of this stratum was continuous with that of the earlier two levels, even though individual forms varied in the frequency of their occurrence. A unique stamp seal of blue frit had a conical back pierced for suspension and a flat face carved with the figure of an animal standing above an unidentifiable figure (Fig. 52).

Stratum D. A major break in the continuity of cultural traditions occurred with the building of City D. Old building lines were completely abandoned. The new plan consisted of two complexes of houses separated by a narrow street (Fig. 43d). In Room 33 there appears the outline of what may have been a potter's kiln, but the wall of its firing chamber had been completely razed. Domestic use of the adjacent house, Room 32, is evidenced by the presence of two baking ovens. The frequent use of ashlar blocks in the walls of City D distinguish it from the poorer construction found in the earlier levels.

Pottery styles as well as building plans and methods display a radical departure from those of the earlier city. The

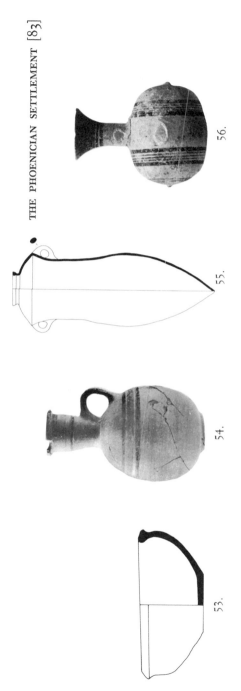

53.

54.

55.

56.

53. Bowl characteristic of Stratum D

54. Red-slip and painted jug

55. Torpedo-shaped amphora from Stratum D

56. Cypriot barrel-shaped jug from Stratum D

shallow platter, which had been the characteristic and dominant type throughout the three earlier periods, was replaced by a new form of bowl (Fig. 53). Red-slip finish appeared on a jug decorated with lines of black and red paint (Fig. 54, for a jug of this type). The fragile rounded storage jar, long popular in the earlier strata, gave way to the sturdier, torpedo-shaped amphora (Fig. 55).

What occasioned these changes? Was the city—or this sector of it—abandoned for a period, during which a change in styles took place gradually at neighboring sites which continued to be occupied? Yet the carefully drawn section (Fig. 42) displays no layer of humus from decayed vegetation or of windblown sand, the usual evidences for a

57. Type of open bowl widely used in Stratum C

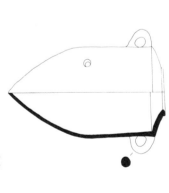

58. Type of amphora characteristic of Stratum C

gap in human occupation. Or, could there have taken place in City D an acceleration of change brought about by contact with the cultures of peoples encountered by the Phoenicians through maritime trade and commerce? There is as yet no conclusive answer.

A date for the abrupt changes which took place in City D is suggested by the presence of a Cypriot jug with a barrel-shaped body in the earlier of the two phases of the stratum (Fig. 56). In her search for Cypriot parallels for the jug, Ellen Herscher has found at Lapithos an example that can be dated to Cypro-Geometric IIIA, a period assigned to the late ninth or early eighth century B.C.

Stratum C. In the plan for City C the former street was utilized for housing and a new one was built at right angles to it (Fig. 43c). The best preserved enclosed area is Room 36, measuring 3.75 m. by 5.20 m. Its walls of well-cut stones and the absence of baking ovens and hearths, which are generally found in domestic areas, suggest the possibility of monumental or public use of this sector of the city at the time of Stratum C.

The ceramic repertory of City C is similar to that of its predecessor, except for a marked increase in the popularity of an open bowl (Fig. 57) which had appeared sporadically in both Strata E and D, and the almost exclusive use of a squat, pointed amphora with a low, plain rim (see Fig. 58 for a complete example of the type found in Stratum B). The latter was to become even more popular in the succeeding period of Stratum B, which belongs to the Hellenistic period.

In summary it can be said that, with the possible exception of the enigmatic discontinuity between City E and City D, there is a continuous development of material culture throughout the period of time represented by these five strata. If the imports of Mycenaean and Cypriot wares are disregarded, a basic unity can be seen within these assemblages of cultural artifacts. Changes there are in the forms of artifacts, but the overall impression is that of a civilization which may properly be termed Phoenician.

The stratified sequence of pottery and other artifacts of everyday life for the Phoenician period from Sounding Y provides a temporal framework in which to place similar objects found in more disturbed contexts. When the evidence from Sounding Y (100 sq. m.) and that from Sounding X (800 sq. m.) are combined, it is possible to reconstruct, in a measure at least, the activities and occupations with which the people of Sarepta concerned themselves throughout the span of the Phoenician period.

Yet the picture of daily life in Phoenicia is limited by two circumstances. First, materials which were widely used have long since decayed without leaving any recognizable trace: wood, textiles, foodstuff, skins. A further limiting factor in the reconstruction is a singular circumstance in the political history of the city. Sarepta apparently enjoyed a peaceful existence throughout the entire Phoenician era of its history. Among the many layers of accumulated debris from human occupation there is lacking a single example of the kind of sudden and total destruction that is characteristic of many ancient cities. There are no deposits of objects of daily life embedded in a layer of ash that resulted from the burning of a city, which forced the inhabitants to flee without their possessions. No such catastrophe, so valuable to the excavator, befell Sarepta. Houses fell into disrepair and their contents were salvaged as new structures were built. Change came, but it was slow and orderly.

Thus for an idea of what the Phoenicians ate, how they dressed and adorned themselves, what crafts they engaged in, how they provided shelter and security—for answers to these and other questions about their general style of life, we must rely on hundreds of artifacts, mostly broken and discarded, as well as upon cautious deductions from the remains of surrounding cultures with which it is reasonable to suppose the inhabitants of Sarepta shared styles and techniques.

Although no cloth has as yet been found, there is tangible

evidence for the spinning of thread, the weaving of thread into textiles, and the sewing which was required to make the cloth into garments. Thread was made by twisting together the fibers of wool—and possibly of flax—and winding it on a spindle of bone or wood, to which was attached a whorl. Dozens of these wheel-like objects cut from stone or bone and pierced with a hole to accommodate the spindle (Fig. 59) attest the making of thread by a process which is well documented on Egyptian tomb paintings and on a bas-relief found at ancient Susa. The only surviving elements of the vertical loom used to weave the thread into cloth are clay weights that were tied to the threads of the warp to keep them taut. They are of two styles. Most common throughout most of the span of Phoenician times is a ball of fired clay, about 8 cm. in diameter, pierced with a hole (Fig. 60); but toward the end of the period weights took the shape of a truncated pyramid, with one of two holes for tying the thread (Fig. 61). That the cloth was sometimes colored by means of a fast dye produced from the extract from a gland of the *murex* may be surmised from the discovery of discarded heaps of shells from this small snail (see p. 126). Long needles of bronze, and also of bone, provided the means for sewing the cloth into garments (Fig. 62). The edges of a loose-fitting garment were fastened together by a fibula, a bronze clasp with a pin attached by a spring to one end, a forerunner of the modern

59. Polished spindle whorl

60. Ball-shaped loom weight

safety-pin (Fig. 63). Bone pins with decorated heads could have served a similar purpose or they could have been worn in the hair for decoration (Figs. 64-66).

Containers for cosmetics and a wide assortment of jewelry bear witness to personal adornment. Two small jars, one of alabaster (Fig. 67) and another of ivory (Fig. 68), are of a type commonly used in Egypt to hold eyepaint; a fragment of one bronze mirror and a decorated bone handle from another (Fig. 69) evidence the use of this toilet article. Beads, found in comparative abundance, may have served as amulets with magical functions as well as jewelry. They are made of clay, stone, faience, frit, and

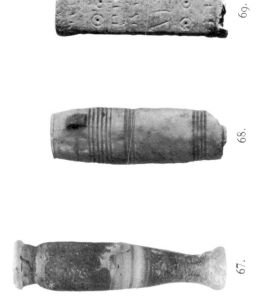

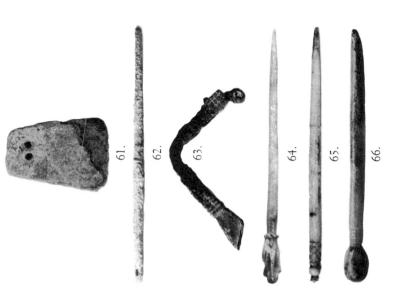

61. Loom weight in shape of truncated pyramid

62. Bronze needle

63. Bronze fibula

64-66. Bone pins with heads decorated with hand-and-ball, pomegranate, and knob

67. Cosmetic jar carved from alabaster

68. Ivory cosmetic jar

69. Bone handle from a mirror

glass, and are fashioned in a variety of shapes. The most distinctive form is that of the glass eye-bead (Fig. 70), which has long been recognized as Phoenician from the many examples which have been found in the colonies established in the West. Pendants, too, were widely used, molded from glass, gold, or faience; Egyptian forms were popular and represented the cat, the baboon, Bes, and the "Eye of Horus" (Fig. 71). Earrings of bronze, silver, or gold (Fig. 72) were worn.

Bread was surely the staple in the diet of the Phoenicians. A hand mill for grinding grain, consisting of a basalt stone with a slightly curved surface on which the grain was crushed by a stone rider (Fig. 73), was widely used. Baking was done in a circular oven shaped like a beehive, with a diameter of from .70 to 1 m. (Fig. 74). The walls were constructed of clay and sometimes covered over with potsherds to provide added insulation. The form of the oven has survived in the *tabun*, which is used for baking today in the village of Sarafand (Fig. 75). Olive pits found in the debris from the Iron Age occupation attest this source for oil and food. Among the animal bones[5] found were those of sheep, goats, oxen, birds, and fish. All of these provided a source of food. A hook of bronze (Fig. 76) has survived to illustrate the method of catching fish.

[5] Identified by Professor Alan Mann of the University Museum.

70. Glass eye-bead

71. "Eye of Horus" pendant

72. Gold earring

73.

74.

75.

73. Basalt grinder with hand grips

74. Two baking ovens in II-A-7, Level 4

75. Clay oven in use at Sarafand

76. Bronze fishhook

77. Horse's head from a clay figurine

78. Rider seated cross-wise on a saddle

79. Bull's head from a figurine

Stews of meat and vegetables were prepared in pots supported by three or more stones over an open fire. Cooking pots, which frequently displayed a deposit of carbon on the outside, have a flaring, grooved rim and are always rounded on the bottom. Their ware is coarse and contains mica grits and large inclusions which allowed the fabric of the pot to expand with increasing heat. Covers for cooking pots were rarely found in Phoenician levels, but it is likely that flat plates were frequently employed as lids. Cooked food was probably eaten from small, deep bowls which could be held easily in the hand. Since no eating utensils were found, such as spoons or forks, one may assume that if such implements were used they were fashioned of wood and have perished.

Many of the artifacts have no obvious utilitarian function. The clay figurines found in the domestic and industrial areas—those recovered from the shrine were essentially different in style—are varied, representing both animal and human figures. Among the more than a dozen crudely fashioned animals, the horse can be identified by the long forelock on the head (Fig. 77); in another example a human rider sits astride what appears to be a horse. Another rider of an animal, possibly a camel, is seated side-wise on a pack saddle (Fig. 78). Curved horns on the head of one figurine suggest that a ram was intended, while another animal displays the horns of a bull

81. Wheel from miniature cart or chariot

80. Charioteer with drawn bow

82. Model boat with apertures for oars or shrouds

83. Weight anchor of stone

(Fig. 79); a short, wide head, although crudely fashioned, may be that of a dog, an animal which is also represented among the skeletal remains. Since animal figurines such as these were lacking among the terracottas found in the shrine, it is unlikely that they were cultic objects. It may well be that the rude representations of domestic animals served as toys for children or as common bric-a-brac for decoration.

Besides the larger animals such as the horse and camel, which were used for riding and presumably for transporting goods, the cart and the boat were used for transporation. A sketch on a sherd depicts a charioteer with drawn bow or shield (Fig. 80); a reined, attenuated animal, most likely a horse to judge from the long tail; and the cart or chariot represented only by its most characteristic feature, a four-spoked wheel. Further evidence for a cart or wagon is to be seen in a terracotta wheel with a projecting hub (Fig. 81), which had belonged to a model, or possibly a toy. Another model in clay is that of a boat, 9.1 cm. long, with pointed bow and stern and sides pierced with holes which could have served to secure shrouds or as openings for oars (Fig. 82). That larger craft were employed is evidenced by a large stone anchor, ca. .60 m. high, in the form of an elongated stone pierced at one end for securing a hawser (Fig. 83). Weight anchors of pierced stone have been found near Mozia, in Sicily, and on Cyprus.

84. Head of a bearded man, from a figurine

85. Head with wide headdress

86. Clay mask with painted beard

87. Upper part of a clay mask with high headdress

Human figurines are predominately female; a head, however, which is all that remains of one, has a short beard (Fig. 84); and another head, with a wide turban (Fig. 85), could also be a male. Yet, with the exception of one figurine with a tambourine, none of the figurines found in the domestic and industrial sections of the city corresponds in type to those which come from the shrine with their emphasis upon aspects of fertility. Such individuality and diversity might be an indication that the crude representations of humans served as toys or as objects designed to satisfy a whim of the maker or to please his customer.

The use to which other objects had been put is even more speculative. Face masks, slightly smaller than life-size, were discovered in various parts of the city. One with a prominent nose and only a slight chin, on which a beard was indicated by black paint, is a caricature (Fig. 86). Others have more normal features. Where the upper part of a mask is preserved, there are oval openings for the eyes through which the wearer could see easily. Since two of the more elaborately decorated masks (Figs. 87 and 88) were found imbedded in the debris of the principal street that ran from the city to the harbor, it is not fanciful to suggest that these terracotta masks were used in processions, possibly on festival days.

Transactions of a business or legal nature were carried out in an orderly and precise fashion. In addition to the

88. Burnished clay mask with beard

89. Stone weight

90. Impression from cylinder seal, with representations of fish on an offering table and other symbols

leaded weight in the form of a heifer, there were two other varieties. One is a polished, round, black stone flattened on the bottom; the other, an oval hematite weight also flattened on one side (Fig. 89). Of the devices used for legalizing contracts or for marking the ownership of property, one is a cylinder seal that could be rolled over a plastic surface (Fig. 90), the other, a stamp seal pierced with a hole so that its owner could carry it suspended by a cord around the neck (Fig. 52).

Among the metal tools and weapons there was a conspicuous dearth of the types of objects usually employed in warfare. There were no spear points. Two dagger pommels, one of iron and another of steatite, were recovered, but there were no examples of a dagger blade. Only six bronze arrowheads were recovered in the entire excavation: two were socketed and had a triple-flanged blade; each of the others had a tang and a flat blade. This meager assemblage of the weapons, when considered with the lack of any general destruction of the city throughout its history, suggests that Sarepta was free from any major threat to its security as it plied its trades in a profitable commerce.

A characteristic building technique used in the construction of house walls is what may be called the pier-and-rubble construction (Fig. 91). Piers or columns of ashlar blocks were first built at intervals of 1 to 1.50 m. along the

91. Wall of pier-and-rubble construction

92. Marginally drafted stones closely fitted together

line which the wall was to follow. The interstices between the piers were then filled with undressed field stones set in clay mortar to complete the wall. Although this method of construction was an economy measure—strength was achieved through the use of easily available field stones— the result presented the pleasing appearance of paneling. Ashlar blocks used in building were sometimes marginally drafted on the exposed face (Fig. 92). A similar treatment of building stones is to be seen in a ninth-century wall uncovered at Samaria in Palestine where, from biblical ac-

counts, Phoenician influence was felt during the reign of Ahab.

From the city plans which we have recovered thus far, it appears that houses were built with their front walls flush with the street. Water from the roof was carried off by the sloping streets, which served as a drainage system as well as for passageways. The accumulation of sediment and gravel on the original surface of a street measured sometimes as much as a meter in depth.

Since no walls have been found standing to their original

rim served to hold the wick in place. However, examples of the two-spouted lamp were found (Fig. 94). It was this type which was widely used in Phoenician colonies.

From the sample of artifacts recovered at Sarepta there emerges a reasonably clear picture of how the average Phoenician lived. Certain elements of Phoenician material culture appear to have originated in their coastal city states and to have been adopted by their Canaanite neighbors in Syria and Palestine and utilized in the colonies established in the West. It would seem likely that the technique for producing red-slip ware was of Phoenician origin. Such construction methods as the pier-and-rubble wall and marginally drafted ashlar blocks appear to have had wide use first in Phoenicia. Yet, with a few exceptions, the elements of Phoenician civilization are those which were shared by the peoples of Syria and Palestine.

What is distinctive about the civilization of the Phoenicians, isolated as they were from the rich agricultural lands which lay behind the Lebanon range, was their development of maritime trade with underdeveloped peoples of the western Mediterranean world. Commerce with these distant markets was made possible by local industries which produced items that could be traded abroad. In a following chapter we shall present the evidence for Phoenician craftsmanship and industry as it appears in one of the coastal cities.

93. Model wall bracket with lamp

94. Two-spouted lamp

height, there is no evidence for the use of windows in houses. Light was provided indoors—perhaps by day as well as by night—by oil lamps placed in a stirrup-like terracotta bracket, which hung from a peg driven into the house wall. Wall brackets were frequent, and one miniature example had a lamp attached to the shelflike projection at the bottom (Fig. 93). Most lamps consisted of a shallow bowl to contain the oil; a pinched segment of the

95. Bowl bearing the name Eshmunyaton

96. Base inscribed with a personal name

VI

The Inscriptions

THE inscriptions found at Sarepta are a source of information about aspects of the culture that cannot be deduced from the anonymous artifacts of daily life. Only a modest sample of writings has survived, but the practiced hand that wrote the names of persons, as well as of the gods propitiated with offerings, attests the wide use of writing. Since the half dozen deities mentioned—Baal, Melqart, Eshmun, Shadrapa, Tanit, Ashtart—are all well documented in other ancient sources as to their attributes and functions, it is possible to obtain from even short or fragmentary inscriptions some indication of the pattern of religious thought and practice of the Sareptans.

Altogether, twenty "documents" were found, varying in length from a single letter incised on a potsherd to a complete, four-line text of thirty-two Phoenician letters cut in ivory. In contrast to most extant Phoenician inscriptions, which were carved on stone for public display, the Sarepta writings, except for two texts, are modest notations incised or painted on ceramic jars or bowls. These letters inscribed on articles of everyday use suggest that writing skill was not restricted to a scribal class but functioned in daily life.

The use of writing for labels on common ceramic ware is strictly limited to the Phoenician period of Sarepta's history. Greek and Latin scripts do appear in the later periods, but their use is restricted to monumental inscriptions, stamps on jar handles from Rhodes, and coins minted elsewhere. Among the thousands of Hellenistic and Roman sherds which were carefully scrutinized, not one bearing an inscription was found.

The provenience of the written material suggests its use in commerce and the cult. All the inscriptions were found in the industrial and religious sector of the city, Sounding X; none came from the section of the city which served as a residential quarter throughout most of its history.

The most frequently recurring word in the inscriptions on pottery is the single letter *l*, meaning "belonging to," or "for." In two instances the preposition is followed by a god's name: Shadrapa is mentioned on one sherd, and the indefinite '*dnm*, "our lord," on another. But human ownership is indicated by the same preposition in one inscription, where it is followed by the personal name Eshmunyaton. In four other fragmentary texts it is impossible to tell whether the *l* denotes ownership by a god or a person.

A close examination of the letters appearing on these sherds that bear a notation of ownership reveals that six out of the seven inscriptions were incised or painted on the surface of the vessel before it was placed in the kiln for firing. Thus, it would appear that the potter had fashioned these jars—most of them for the storage of some commodity—either for a particular client or as a container for an offering to be made at the shrine of a deity.

In general the identifying label had been placed where it could be readily seen. However, there are two exceptions. The inscription "belonging to Eshmunyaton" had been inscribed with a sharp instrument on the under side of a large bowl so that it could not be seen unless the dish was turned upside down (Fig. 95). The other unobtrusive legend inscribed on the bottom of a jar reads . . . *sh bn 'b . . . , ". . . SH son of 'B . . . ,*" but unfortunately only the last two letters of the man's name and the first two letters of his father's are preserved on this fragment of a base (Fig. 96).

The longest inscription incised on pottery consisted of 20 letters on a sherd, measuring 8 by 9 cm., from a large, salmon-colored storage jar (Fig. 97).[1] Both ends of each of the two lines are missing. The writing, which had been

[1] Javier Teixidor has provided notes and bibliographic references for this, the Shadrapa and the Sarepta inscriptions in his chapter, "Selected Inscriptions," which appeared in my *Sarepta: A Preliminary Report on the Iron Age*, 1975, pp. 97-104. Ref-

done before firing, is in a style generally used in inscriptions of the fifth and fourth century B.C.

Transliterating the consonants and changing the direction—Phoenician was written from right to left—they read:

$$\ldots hwzh\dot{t}y \ldots$$

$$\ldots 'mr\ l\ 'dnn \cdot grmlqr[t] \ldots$$

A man's name appears at the end of the second line and is complete except for the final *t*. Supplying the missing vowels—they are never written in Phoenician but had to be supplied as in modern speed-writing—the name is Germelqart. Three other Phoenicians are known to have borne this name: in Byblos there was found a jar stamped with Germelqart, and two stelae from Cyprus record the use of the name in the Phoenician settlement there. As colonies were founded and grew in the West, the name Germelqart came to be widely used.

This popular name is actually a phrase composed of two words, *ger* and Melqart, "client of Melqart." Furthermore, the name Melqart, a god of Tyre, is also a phrase meaning "king of the city," an epithet of a god who was commonly referred to by his principal title. As Phoenicians from Tyre

erence to Teixidor's first study of these inscriptions will make apparent my debt to him for many of the interpretations found on these pages.

went to Cyprus and Carthage they took their city's god, who in time became popular in the colonies.

Not only did Germelqart bear the Tyrian god's name, but it would seem from the inscription that he himself was religiously observant. The second line of the inscription is a dedication of an offering made to his god, who is referred to as '*dnn*, "our lord," a deity so well known that the dedicator did not feel obliged to be more specific.

The kind of offering which Germelqart presented to his lord is indicated by the first word of the line, '*mr*, "lamb." The same word appears in a Punic inscription on a votive stela found at el-Hofra in Constantine, North Africa. But in this dedication it is combined with *mlk*, a name for a specific Canaanite offering made at the Tophet near Jerusalem (II Kings 23:10). In the Punic text Akborat is said to have vowed a vow and presented a *mlk* '*mr* "for the lord, for Ba'al Hammon" (*ANET³*, 658). Despite the fragmentary condition of the line in the Sarepta inscription, the meaning is clear: Germelqart presented to his lord a characteristic Canaanite offering in a jar which had been fabricated for the purpose.

The line above the dedicatory formula is more difficult to understand, although the six letters are so clearly inscribed that there can be no question about the identification of each one of them. But no Phoenician word or words are spelled in that way. Together these letters made no sense until it was recalled that these letters were in

97. Inscription of Germelqart

precisely the same order as those of the Hebrew alphabet as it is known from acrostic Psalms (111, 112, 145).

One would have thought that among the many Phoenician inscriptions that have come to light there should have been one at least that recorded the traditional order of the letters in the alphabet. Yet until the recovery of this fragment at Sarepta no Phoenician abecedary had been found. One could have guessed with reasonable certainty the Phoenician sequence from three tablets found at Ras Shamra which document the order of the older and somewhat longer alphabet of Ugaritic.[2] There the six letters of our text, hwzḥty, appear in the same sequence although the script in which they are written is entirely different. Through the nine centuries which separate the writing of our fragment from that of the text from Ugarit the traditional order of at least these six letters had been maintained.

Was the potter (or Gemelqart) merely making a show of his erudition by inscribing his jar with ABC's? Was he practicing writing the alphabet? Or did the alphabet have some religious or magical significance? We do not know the answer, but he did bequeath to us an unique example of a part, at least, of an abecedary in the Phoenician script. Another dedicatory inscription contains the actual name

of the god for whom the gift was intended (Fig. 98). Eight letters and part of a ninth are inscribed in a practiced hand of the fifth century B.C. on a sherd from the shoulder of a large, salmon-colored storage jar which had been decorated with two grooves above the inscription and a band below burnished to a high polish. Obviously it was not an ordinary container. The first six letters, lšdrp', are certainly to be read as "for Shadrapa." These are followed by the conjunction w and a š, obviously the beginning of the name of another deity to whom, along with Shadrapa, the jar or its contents was dedicated. It is clear from the smoothness of the strokes of the writing instrument and from the clay that remains gouged out at the end of the incisions that the jar had been inscribed before the potter had placed it in the kiln for firing.

Only once before had the name Shadrapa been discovered in the Phoenician homeland. On a stela from Amrit, which has been variously dated from the ninth to the fifth century, the name is faintly legible in a dedication incised between the tail and the head of the lion (Fig. 99). In an Egyptianized representation the god stands confidently on the back of a lion, which strides through a mountainous terrain. The god's supremacy over the lion is further suggested by his grasp of the hind legs of a cub

[2] For references to the Ugaritic and other alphabets see M. D. Coogan, *Bulletin of the American Schools of Oriental Research*, 216, 1974, pp. 61-63.

98. The Shadrapa inscription

99. The Amrit stela with dedication to Shadrapa

in his left hand. If the figure on the Amrit stela is indeed that of the god Shadrapa, he is clearly in control of that ferocious and feared beast, the lion.

Further particulars about Shadrapa may be inferred from a representation of him found at Palmyra. An inscribed stela, dated to A.D. 55, now in the British Museum (Fig. 100), depicts the deity as a mailed warrior holding a spear, around which a serpent is entwined; a scorpion grasps harmlessly at his shoulder.[3] Obviously Shadrapa is in control here of these two chthonic enemies of mankind and when they are considered along with the lions of the Amrit stela, erected to Shadrapa, it seems clear that this god controlled all these hostile forces. Nor is the evidence for Shadrapa's association with serpents and scorpions confined to the stela from Palmyra. There have also been found at Palmyra a dozen tesserae stamped with representations of scorpions and snakes, and occasionally the name šdrpʾ.[4]

The wide diffusion of the worship of Shadrapa is well documented at Punic sites. A fourth-third century B.C. base for a statue has been found at Antas in Sardinia, inscribed with a dedication of a statue of Shadrapa to the god Şid. In Sicily on the wall of a cave, Grotta Regina, on the coast

[3] H. Ingholt, *Studier over palmyrensk Skulptur*, 1928, 19, pl. I, 1; *Berytus*, 3, 1936, pp. 137-39.

[4] J. Starcky, *Syria*, 26, 1949, pp. 67-81.

100. Representation of Shadrapa on a stela from Palmyra

at Cape Gallo, someone had painted a blessing for Shadrapa. Both Carthage and Leptis Magna in North Africa have yielded inscriptions in which the god is mentioned. On a bilingual inscription from Leptis Magna, Shadrapa is equated with Liber Pater, the Italian god of fertility. In the East the name persisted and is found as late as the sixth century A.D. at the Babylonian site of Nippur. An Aramaic text inscribed on a bowl mentions Shadrapa as one of the angels "who bring salvation to all the children of men." Shadrapa had survived for more than a millennium in the ancient Near East.[5]

The name of a Phoenician god of healing appears as the theophorous element in the name Eshmunyaton, "Eshmun has given," which we have mentioned above (p. 98) as having been incised on the underside of a large bowl. Only a few miles to the north, at Sidon, the cult of healing is well attested at the temple of Eshmun, which has been excavated by M. Maurice Dunand. There this healing god and Asclepius, with whom he was identified in later times, received votive offerings for the cures sought from these deities. It is not surprising, therefore, to encounter the name of Eshmun, the healer, in a personal name at the nearby Sarepta.

[5] A. Dupont-Sommer, in *Comptes rendus de l'Académie des Inscriptions et Belles-Lettres*, 1974, pp. 146-47, suggests an Iranian origin for the god Shadrapa.

102. Drawing of an impression from the Sarepta stamp

101. Stamp bearing the name Sarepta

Among the inscribed objects discovered it was the smallest that provided the crucial evidence for linking the archaeological remains at Sarafand with the ancient city of Sarepta long known from historical sources. The face of a scarab-shaped, greenish-brown stone, which measured 1.9 cm. in length, bears three lines of Phoenician letters which had been cut in reverse—mirror writing—so that when the stamp was impressed on a plastic surface the writing would appear as it was conventionally read (Figs. 101-102 for the stamp and a drawing of the impression). It was pierced longitudinally for a cord that went around the neck or wrist of the owner, or for the mounting of a ring.

In the first line of the inscription two letters, 'š, are clear but the third has been damaged by a break in the stone. Shortly after the discovery of the Sarepta seal there appeared on the antiquity market in Beirut an unbroken seal of the same shape which has in the first of three lines of Phoenician writing the word 'šr, and in the second the name of Achshaph ('kšp), a city which is mentioned in Joshua 11:1. From this analogous example it is likely that 'šr was the reading of the first line of our seal. Yet the meaning of these three letters is far from clear. While one might expect a personal name in the first line of a stamp seal, no Phoenician or Punic name employing these letters is known. In Hebrew these three consonants are used as a verb meaning "to tithe." Thus, there is the possibility that

the word on the seal has to do with the collection of dues or taxes. Since a council of ten is known to have been in charge of religious matters in Carthage and at Palmyra "the Ten" bore responsibility for the payment of taxes, Javier Teixidor, who has published a study of this inscription, has suggested with reservation that the line might designate "the Ten," a college or committee of ten which ruled in Sarepta. But there is as yet no evidence for the political system at Sarepta.

The third line is as enigmatic as the first. Teixidor reads the first letter as ', and considers it as an abbreviation for the name of a king. In fact, about 400 B.C., Sidon had a king whose name began with an 'ayin, (King) 'b'mn. The abbreviation is followed by the number 12, that is, the twelfth year of the monarch.

Although the first and third lines present problems of reading and interpretation, the second line is clearly *ṣrpt*, the four letters of the Phoenician city of Sarepta, spelled as it is in the celebrated story of Elijah's visit in I Kings 17:9. The name appears in the same position on the seal as does the name of the city Achshaph on the *'šr* seal of unknown provenience in Beirut.

What use had been made of this seal in the late fifth century B.C., to which it is to be dated by the form of its letters? Most likely it had served for stamping handles of amphorae with a label which gave the source and the date of the product which they were to contain. Yet among the thousands of amphora handles found in the course of the excavation not one bore an impression of this stamp or of one like it. A plausible explanation for the absence of stamped jar handles is that the stamping was reserved for jars that were exported, a theory that would explain why the city's name was on the stamp.

Despite the lack of evidence for how the seal was used in the commerce of the city, the discovery does confirm the guess which has been made repeatedly over the past two centuries by Pococke, Robinson, Renan, and others, that the modern Arabic name of Sarafand has preserved the essential consonants of the ancient Sarepta.

103. The inscribed ivory plaque

The longest of the Phoenician inscriptions and the only completely preserved text consists of 32 letters incised on an ivory plaque, measuring 3·3 by 5 cm. (Fig. 103). The inscription serves to identify a cult practiced at Sarepta and to provide an answer to a longstanding question about the origin of the principal goddess of Carthage.

Phoenician inscriptions on ivory are extremely rare and those which have been found previously have come from such distant sites as Nimrud in Assyria, Samaria in Palestine, and Arslan Tash in northern Syria, not from

Phoenicia proper. They consist of a word or phrase in Phoenician on an inlay for furniture, or merely of a single letter on the side or back of the ivory inlay to aid the craftsman in fitting the piece within the panel.

The only other Phoenician inscription on ivory of a length comparable to that of the Sarepta plaque is on an inlay for the top of a box found at Ur by Leonard Woolley[6] While there are gaps in the two-line text, it is clear that the box and likely what was in it were the gift of a certain lady, 'Amat-Ba'al, to her goddess Ashtart.

That the Sarepta plaque served quite a different function is apparent from the first word of the text, which describes the object to which the label had been attached. The word with which the inscription begins, *sml*, is a common designation in Phoenician, Punic, and Hebrew for "image" or "statue." But in Phoenician the same noun is also used in a feminine form—a *t* was added—apparently when the statue was that of a female. It is likely, therefore, that the image referred to was the representation of a male.

We can only speculate as to the material used for the statue. If the sculptor had worked with stone, bronze, or clay, he would have found a smooth surface ready at hand for inscribing his dedication and the statue would

likely have survived along with the inscription. But if the medium in which the artisan worked was wood, it would only have been natural for him to follow the well-documented fashion of inlaying wood with ivory.

That wood was, in fact, used for images in the Canaanite cult we know from the account of Gideon's iconoclasm—he cut down the *'asherah* and burnt it (Judges 6:25-26)—and from Pliny's remark about Phoenician cedar. "Its actual timber," he wrote, "lasts forever, and consequently it has been the regular practice to use it even for making statues of the gods" (*Natural History* 13.11.53, trans. from Loeb ed.). If the missing statue had been of wood, which seems probable, it would have turned to dust after 2600 years, despite Pliny's optimistic estimate of its durability.

The reading of the letters of the text is fairly clear:

hsml ᵓz pᶜ
l šlm bn m
p ᶜl bn ᶜzy l
tnt ᶜštrt

"The statue which Shillem, son of Mapaᶜal, son of ᶜIzai made for Tanit ᶜAshtart."[7]

---

[6] *Antiquaries Journal*, 7, 1927, pl. 49:1.
[7] It is possible to read *hsml ᵓz* as "this statue." Cf. H. Donner and W. Röllig, *Kanaanäische und aramäische Inschriften* (hereafter: KAI), I-III, 1966-1969, 24:15, where the article and

Although there is a question as to how one letter, or possibly two, in the personal name of the maker of the statue is to be read, there can be little doubt about the reading of the last line, "Tanit 'Ashtart," the two goddesses to whom it was dedicated. This short text would occasion no surprise in its eastern context were it not for the dedication to the goddess Tanit, which has hitherto been found only in the western colonies, never in the homeland.

Tanit has long been known from several thousand Carthaginian stelae, inscribed with dedications to her and to Baal Hammon and frequently bearing a symbol which has come to be known as the "Sign of Tanit." The context in which these stelae have been found has suggested an association of this goddess with the Punic cult of child sacrifice. Reporting on his discovery at Carthage in 1925 of about 1,100 funerary urns, many of them containing the charred bones of young children, along with stelae dedicated to Tanit, Francis W. Kelsey asked, "Who was this potent goddess Tanit?" In answer he ventured an opinion which has been echoed many times over during the past half century: "Tanit is distinctly Carthaginian, and may represent a primitive Libyan divinity, whose cult, blending with Phoenician elements, was taken over by the Phoenician colony."[8]

Statements that child sacrifice had been practiced in Carthage have long been available in the writings of Diodorus of Sicily and other Greek and Roman writers. But the discovery of the infant burial ground at Carthage, called a *tophet* (after the name used in Jeremiah 7:31 for the place of child sacrifice in Jerusalem), provided a concrete illustration of this practice of Punic religion. With the excavation of other Punic sites in the western Mediterranean it became apparent that human sacrifice was not limited to Carthage but had been practiced at Sousse in North Africa, Mozia in Sicily, and Monte Sirai, Tharros, Nora, and Sulcis in Sardinia.[9] Thus the *tophet*, with which Tanit is related by inscriptions with dedications to her

demonstrative are both used (see J. Friedrich and W. Röllig, *Phönizisch-Punische Grammatik*, 1970, p. 300, for other examples of this syntax). However, I prefer considering 'z as a relative (Friedrich and Röllig, p. 293), since in our inscription there seems to be a word-divider between the noun and relative, which would serve to make the relative 'z proclitic to the verb, as it is in *KAI*, 1:1 (see Z. S. Harris, *A Grammar of the Phoeni-*

cian *Language*, 1936, p. 55, for other examples of this use).

[8] *Excavations at Carthage 1925: A Preliminary Report*, 1926, p. 50.

[9] S. Moscati, "Il sacrificio dei fanciulli," *Rendiconti della Pontificia Accademia Romana di Archaeologia*, 38, 1965-66, pp. 61-68.

(and to Baal Hammon), has become a hallmark of Punic religion.

Our Sarepta inscription contains the first unequivocal occurrence of Tanit in the Phoenician homeland in the East, but there were some hints, even before its discovery that she might have had a Phoenician origin. A stela of remembrance discovered in Athens as long ago as 1795 mentions a certain 'Abdtanit as a Sidonian.[10] When an inscription containing the phrase "Tanit in *lbmn*" was found in Carthage in 1898, scholars generally took the *lbmn* as referring to a "white" (*lbn*) hill on which the temple of Tanit, mentioned in the text, had been built.[11] They found it impossible to read the name as the Syrian Lebanon. And in 1964-1965, M. Dunand discovered at Eshmun, near Sidon, an ostrakon of the fifth century containing a list of names, among which was Gertanit.[12] But such well-known scholars as Dussaud, Lidzbarsky, Röllig, Gsell, and Charles-Picard had assigned Tanit to an African origin rather than to a Phoenician one.

While the importance of the inscription is primarily chronological and geographic—it is the earliest preserved mention of the Carthaginian goddess and the first evidence for her cult in the homeland of the Phoenicians—it is unique for yet another reason. The name of the best known of all Phoenician ladies, Ashtart, is associated with her. But the laconic "for Tanit Ashtart" is subject to two interpretations.

The first is that by the seventh century B.C. the cult of Tanit had been joined to that of Ashtart. Such syncretism is suggested by compounds like Mulk-Ashtart, Eshmun-Ashtart, Sid-Tanit, Reshef-Mekal, Reshef-Melqart, Sid-Melqart, and Eshmun-Melqart. The second interpretation is more probable: there is an implied conjunction between the two divine names. The dedication is to Tanit (and) Ashtart, both of whom were served at the same shrine.[13]

With the appearance in Canaanite Phoenicia of the goddess Tanit, who is linked with child sacrifice in the West, the several condemnations by Hebrew writers of those who "burn their sons and their daughters in the fire," (Jeremiah 7:31-32, 19:3-6; II Kings 23:10) take on new credibility as a description of a widespread cultic practice in the Levant.

The letters *tnt* on the dedicatory plaque were not the only evidence for Tanit at Sarepta. The "Sign of Tanit," so frequently found associated with the name of the goddess on stelae from the Punic world, appears on a molded disk of glass, 1 cm. in diameter, which could have served as an inset for a ring or other ornament (Fig. 104). The

[10] *KAI*, 53.
[11] *KAI*, 81.

[12] *Bulletin du Musée de Beyrouth*, 20, 1967, pp. 47-55, pl. 1.
[13] At Carthage Tanit and Ashtart had shrines (*KAI*, 81).

simple design, composed of a triangle and a circle separated by a horizontal bar with upturned ends, has been variously interpreted—a worshiper with upraised hands, a betyl and sun disk, an anchor which was the insignia of Tyre, a modification of the Egyptian ankh-sign—but strong evidence has been recently adduced to show that the sign is a stylized form of a female figure and that the term "Sign of Tanit" is not inappropriate for this enigmatic design. Not only has the "Sign of Tanit" been found at Sarepta, but also at two other sites on the Phoenician coast. In 1973 the emblem was found at Acco stamped on a sherd from a storage jar.[14] Not far away at Haifa, Elisha Linder salvaged from the cargo of a fifth-century ship wrecked off the coast a cache of terracotta figurines, some of which were stamped with the familiar "Sign of Tanit."[15] The stamped emblem on female figurines adds further support to the explanation mentioned above that the geometric figure represents the goddess herself.

That the Phoenician alphabet had been used at Sarepta occasioned no surprise since examples of this form of writing had long been known from the coastal cities of Tyre, Sidon, and Byblos. What was entirely unexpected at

[14] M. Dothan, "A Sign of Tanit from Tel 'Akko," *Israel Exploration Journal,* 24, 1974, pp. 44-49.
[15] *Archaeology,* 26, 1973, pp. 182-87.

104. Glass disk bearing the "Sign of Tanit"

Sarepta was evidence for the use of the Ugaritic script, an alphabet of cuneiform symbols which had been widely used at the coastal site of Ras Shamra. Ugaritic had been attested by occasional texts from such inland sites in Palestine as Taanach, Tabor, and Beth Shemesh, and a three-letter inscription had been found at Kamid el-Loz in the Biqa' Valley,[16] but until 1972 there had been no Ugaritic writing found at any of the coastal Phoenician sites to the south of Ras Shamra.

The inscription is almost complete, written in two lines on a large, five-ribbed handle from an amphora (Figs. 105 and 106). Unlike Phoenician, which is written from right to left, the Ugaritic text runs from left to right as is the

[16] G. Wilhelm, "Eine Krughenkelinschrift in alphabetischer Keilscrift aus Kāmid el-Lōz," *Ugarit Forschungen,* 5, 1973, pp. 284-85.

106. Drawing of the Ugaritic inscription

105. Ugaritic inscription on a ribbed jar handle

general practice in the texts from Ras Shamra. The alphabet was not drawn or scratched but the signs were made by impressing a stylus in plastic clay—an age-old practice developed first in Mesopotamia and used in the writing of Sumerian and then employed for Babylonian and Assyrian.

Fifteen letters are clearly impressed in this manner, but one, the second in the first line, is drawn in a cursive fashion and bears no likeness to any known form of the Ugaritic alphabet. It does, however, bear some resemblance to a Phoenician g inscribed in reverse. If one assumes that for some reason the writer employed this Phoenician form of the letter g—he could not recall the Ugaritic form, or the Phoenician alphabet had at the time begun to replace the Ugaritic—then the word of which it is a part is intelligible in the text. The noun 'agn is attested in Ugaritic as "jar" or "ewer." Making use of this guess about the strange letter, we are able to read the two lines, both of which are missing a letter at the beginning and at the end, as:

['ʾ]agn / pʿl yd[y]
[ʿ]bl / lḥdṯ bʿ[l]

The slashes represent the vertical lines drawn for some

unknown reason between certain words or phrases. David I. Owen, who prepared the notes for the preliminary report in the first publication, considers the meaning to be:[17]

(This) ewer, the work of my hands,
ʿObal made for (the festival ? of) the new moon.

The translation "work of my hands" for the phrase pʿl ydy, which, while not attested in Ugaritic, is supported

[17] For bibliographical references see the notes of David I. Owen in my Sarepta: A Preliminary Report on the Iron Age, 1975, pp. 102-4. See arguments of E. L. Greenstein that the language of the text is Phoenician, The Journal of the Ancient Near Eastern Society of Columbia University, 8, 1976, pp. 49-57.

by the appearance of the phrase in the Old Testament (Isa. 45:11; cf. Deut. 33:11), which in numerous passages displays a remarkable similarity to the vocabulary of the Canaanite texts from Ugarit. The name of the maker of the jar, 'Obal, which, although it lacks the first of its three consonants in our text, is also a name which is found in the Bible in two contexts (Gen. 10:28 and I Chron. 1:22) as well as in a text from Ugarit itself.[18] More problematical is the reading "the new moon," which could also be construed as a personal name, Ḥudashi, which is known from Ugarit.

An approximate date of the beginning of the thirteenth century for the inscription was supplied by the Carbon-14 analysis of charred wood found within a room adjoining that in which the jar handle was discovered (see pp. 121-23). This date falls within the period of the fourteenth and thirteenth centuries when Ugaritic is known to have been used.

After surveying the limited amount of written material found in the ruins of Sarepta and attempting to extract information from proper names about such matters as foreign connections and religion, one may ask why more

18 Javier Teixidor has called my attention to the evidence given by J. T. Milik, Recherches d'épigraphie proche-orientale I, Dédicaces faites par des dieux (Palmyre, Hatra, Tyr) et des

Phoenician writing has not survived. At a seaport, with cargoes moving across the quays, records would surely have been kept of shipments. Where are the commercial records of this maritime people? The discoveries at Ras Shamra demonstrate that the fourteenth-century merchants of Ugarit wrote inventories on clay tablets and baked them in kilns for a permanent record. One would expect to find similar records in the Phoenician script at a port like Sarepta.

A possible answer is that the Phoenicians had discovered the advantages of papyrus over clay as a writing material. Evidence that the Prince of Byblos received papyrus from Egypt as a payment for cedar is preserved in the tale of the eleventh-century Wen-Amon (p. 24). While clay provided a surface into which a Ugaritic scribe could impress his alphabet of wedge-shaped symbols, the more cursive letters of the Phoenician alphabet could be more readily written with ink on a sheet of papyrus. The storage of records on papyrus rolls would have been easier than those on the bulkier material of clay tablets. What was lost, however, in this change from the use of clay tablets to papyrus as writing material was the permanence of the record.

thiases sémitiques à l'époque romaine, 1972, pp. 108-9, that 'gn came to mean a religious banquet or symposium at Palmyra.

VII

The Industrial Quarter

WHEN it became clear that there were Phoenician remains within the 10 m. square of Sounding X, chosen to test the stratigraphy of the mound at Ras el-Qantara, this limited area was enlarged toward the north, west, and south—an ash heap lay to the east—to include eventually a total of 800 sq. m. (Fig. 107). It became apparent upon reaching bedrock that this part of the city had never been a typical living area. Domestic architecture was conspicuously absent. There were no bins for the storage of foodstuff, a facility commonly found in housing areas; and the few baking ovens and domestic hearths which did appear were situated at the very edge, not at the heart, of the area.

In place of these more common remains of ancient occupation there emerged installations and objects which could be associated with more specialized activities. This section of the city had been given over to industry for about a millennium of its archaeological history. Potters, pressers of olives, dyers, and metalworkers had practiced their crafts and trades. The only exception to this commercial use of the district was the construction of a small

shrine sometime in the eighth-seventh century B.C., a building which will be described in Chapter VIII. Sounding X was primarily the industrial quarter of Sarepta.

One can only speculate about the reason for the continued specialized use of one sector of the city through so many centuries. Was the industrial quarter placed where it was because of the advantage which proximity to the harbor afforded? Were the prevailing winds which blew over the promontory on which the kilns were located useful in the firing process? Or, was this land originally owned by potters and other craftsmen who passed along to successive generations both their land and their skills? The answer must await the further recovery of the city's plan and more evidence for the organization of its society.

Pottery-making is the most fully documented among the several crafts and industries for which evidence has been found. Spread over this relatively small area of about one-fifth of an acre were the remains of 22 kilns which had been used in various periods. Tanks for washing and wedging clay, open courts equipped with basins for containing the slip used in decorating the surface of vessels,

107. View of the industrial quarter as it appeared in the 1972 season from a tethered balloon

had been cut by the digging of a second firing chamber from the upper level of the debris which had covered it. The second kiln was in turn displaced by a third; the third, by a fourth; and finally a fifth structure (Kiln C-D) was built as the last in the sequence within this relatively small area of the industrial sector. Obviously potters had held tenaciously to this particular property.

The first kilns at Sarepta were constructed according to a plan which remained standard for centuries. Only the shape and dimensions changed slightly. Typical of the earliest kilns—those resting on bedrock—is Kiln S, which was found in the square II-D-6 (Fig. 108). Except for its east wall, which lay beyond the limits of the excavation, the plan of the firing chamber was complete.

The plan is that of an oval chamber divided into two kidney-shaped lobes by a wall that projects from the side opposite to the doorway. On the inside the chamber measures 2.40 m. in width and 4.40 m. along the long axis. A doorway, .80 m. wide, leads into the constricted neck of the bottle-shaped structure and provided the opening through which the fuel used in the firing was introduced. During the first phase of the use of this kiln the fieldstone walls had been lined with a coating of clay, which had turned to a brick-red color during the firing process. In a subsequent period of use, however, the walls had been lined with small limestone blocks set in mortar

potter's tools, and heaps of sherds from vessels which had been discarded because of cracking, blistering, warping, or explosion in the kiln during firing—these bore evidence for the continued use of the area by potters and document the technology of what was the most extensively practiced craft of the ancient world. At no other pre-Greek site in the eastern Mediterranean have so many kilns been found.

How many more kilns there are beyond the limits of the 20 by 40 m. area of Sounding X it is impossible to tell. Yet three partly excavated kilns along the eastern limit of the excavation indicate that the ceramic industry extended farther to the east, and a kiln (Kiln AA) that showed in the west balk of Sounding Y, lying some 100 m. to the southwest, could have belonged to the same industrial complex. Thus there may well have been as many as a hundred kilns in the industrial area; and at any one time a dozen furnaces may have sent forth columns of smoke from the brush and wood with which workmen fed them.

The 22 kilns which were recovered in Sounding X belonged to various periods of occupation. In one 10 by 15 m. area (II-B/C-4/6) it was possible to determine the sequence of five kilns through overlapping or other indications of stratigraphy. The earliest, with its base directly on bedrock, had fallen into disuse and part of the structure

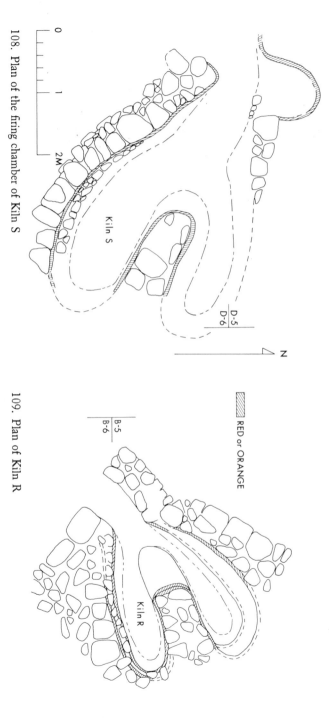

108. Plan of the firing chamber of Kiln S

and these had been partly turned to lime by intense heat. Most of the kilns of both the early and the later periods had been coated inside with layers of clay—sometimes as many as ten layers could be counted in section—which had fired to a hardness of brick.

109. Plan of Kiln R

A similar plan was used in the construction of Kiln R, in II-B-5/6 (Fig. 109). It too had been repaired and re-used many times, but the lining of its walls was exclusively of clay, which had proved to be more durable than limestone. Kiln R was slightly smaller than Kiln S, meas-

0 1 2M

RED or ORANGE

Kiln S

D-5
D-6

N

B-5
B-6

Kiln R

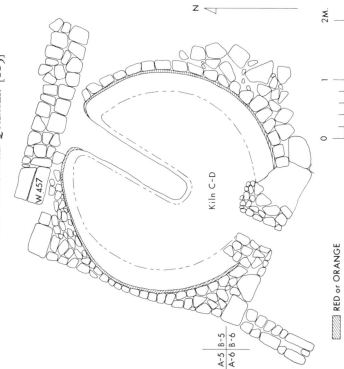

Kiln C-D

N

0   1   2 M.

A-5 | B-5
A-6 | B-6

RED or ORANGE

110. Plan of Kiln C-D

uring 1.80 by 3.40 m. As in Kiln S, the tongue-like wall that divided the kiln's chamber was wide, occupying approximately a third of the floor space within the kiln.

The plan of the earlier kilns was eventually superseded by a new design. Overlying Kiln R, in squares II-B-5/6, was found the well-preserved outline of its successor, Kiln C-D (Fig. 110). The characteristic feature of a tongue projecting from the back wall has been maintained, although reduced in width, but the shape of the kiln has been altered from long oval to circular. There is no neck-like passage from the doorway to the firing chamber, and the entrance has been constricted to a mere .30 m. Its walls, where preserved, are built of brick (Fig. 111), which provided good insulation and did not disintegrate under heat as did limestone. The same circular plan was followed in the construction of the two Kilns E and F (p. 123), the latter lying above an oval-shaped kiln in II-B-8. From the chronological sequence established by the stratigraphy of the kilns, it is clear that the earlier elliptical shape was displaced in the later periods by a circular plan.

Kilns vary markedly in size. The width of the smallest (Kiln J, not illustrated) is 1.30 m. and that of the largest, Kiln C-D, is 3.80 m. Doorways vary in width from .30 m. to .90 m., but the majority of those with remaining entranceways fall within the range of from .40 m. to .50 m. There is no uniformity of pattern for the orientation of

111. Firing chamber of Kiln C-D

the openings to the firing chamber. Apparently the kilns were constructed without taking into account the direction of the prevailing winds.

By the end of the 1971 season four kilns had been discovered, but none was preserved to a height of more than a meter above the floor. Early in the 1972 campaign there appeared in II-C-8 a segment of an arc of bricklike material perforated with five holes. These seemed to be flues in the top of a kiln that had survived intact (Fig. 112). When the structure, called Kiln G, was excavated it became apparent that at least one kiln had been preserved with a complete firing chamber, a roof with flues, and a doorway leading to a stoking room from which it had been fired. The fortunate discovery of this well-preserved kiln provided answers to questions about the ceramic technology employed at Sarepta. It is, in fact, one of the best-preserved examples of an ancient pre-Greek kiln yet to appear in the Near East. The only missing element in Kiln G is the upper chamber in which the vessels were stacked for firing.

The kiln had been worked from two levels. The upper level consisted of an open courtyard, Room 74, where the potter had fashioned clay into pots, set them out to dry, and then stacked them in the upper chamber of the kiln (Fig. 113). At a level of about a meter and a half below the courtyard was the stoking room for the firing chamber,

112. Flues for the firing chamber of Kiln G

an area in which fuel was stored and ashes from the fire collected at the end of the firing process.

The method used in the construction of the kiln eventually became clear. First, an oblong pit had been dug through the layers of earlier occupation to a depth of about 1.50 m. When the excavation was completed, a U-shaped wall, averaging .60 m. in width, was built of fieldstones flush against the sides of the pit to form the firing chamber (Fig. 114). The inside of the wall had a smooth face; the outside was rough and uneven since the stones had been merely packed against the sides of the

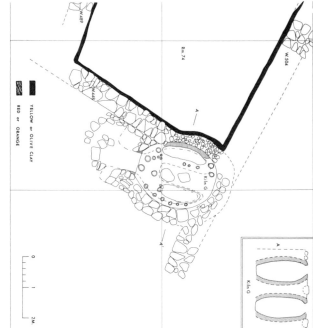

113. Plan and section of Kiln G

114. Kiln G viewed from the stoking room to the south

excavation. A wall was then constructed on the long axis of the oval chamber from the back toward the entrance-way for about two-thirds of the length of the kiln. This tongue-like projection served as a support for an arched roof, which was from .30 to .40 m. thick, built up of layers of plastic clay. Clay was plastered on the sides of the concave walls of the two lobes of the firing chamber to a thickness of from .12 to .16 m. to provide insulation.

The maximum internal measurements of the firing chamber are 1.85 by 2.40 m. and the roof stands at a height of from 1.30 to 1.36 m. above the floor. Perforating the roof are 33 flues or vents (two segments of the roof which had collapsed had probably contained additional flues). Exposure to the elements had eroded the upper surface of the roof, but the orifices of the flues had withstood the deterioration better since the passage of flames and hot gasses had fired them into a harder material. The original surface of the roof, which had served as a floor for the stacking room, had been smooth. The smaller flues from the firing chamber are vertical; but around the perimeter of the roof larger flues, about .12 m. in diameter, had been fashioned so as to extend obliquely outward from the chamber below. Obviously the larger flues served to deflect the hot gasses from the fire to the sides of the stacking room and thus to distribute the heat more evenly to the pots.

The entrance into the kiln's firing chamber consists of a passageway, about a meter long, leading from the stoking area to the chamber. Although no evidence for its upper portion remained, the corridor was presumably roofed over. At the south end of the passageway there was a semicircle of stones, partly embedded in the floor, which appeared to have served as a fender for the fire, or possibly as a barrier to contain the accumulated ash.

The last firing left a deposit of from .10 to .12 m. of greenish-black ash on the floor of the chamber, and there remained a temporary wall which had been built to block the doorway for the purpose of controlling the rate of combustion within the chamber. By closing the draft from below, and perhaps by plugging some of the flues above with stones (some of which were found in place), it had been possible to reduce the heat gradually within the kiln and prevent the cracking of vessels from sudden changes in temperature.

The entire area of the stoking room to the east of wall 448 was filled with ash and other burned material that extended, as could be seen from the balk, southward beyond the limits of the excavation. Wall 448 was a terrace wall separating the two levels from which the kiln was operated.

On the upper level a rectangular area, 6.40 by 7.60 m., was identified by the remains of potter's clay, which cov-

115. Potter's workshop in the courtyard to the west of Kiln G

was a circular basin with a diameter of *ca.* 1.50 m., which was cut into the floor to a depth of from .15 to .18 m. It could have served to work the clay or to contain slip, which was applied to the surface of a leather-hard vessel as a decoration. In the workshop of a later period a basin of similar dimensions was found, but it had been coated with a layer of cement (Fig. 116). Besides a considerable quantity of potsherds, three small goblets and a complete amphora (Fig. 117) were found on the floor of the working area. Since a portion of the clay-lined east wall of Room 74 was also the west wall of Kiln G, there can be little doubt about the association of the potter's working area with the kiln. Pots fashioned in the potter's working area could easily be lifted about a half meter to the level of the floor of the adjacent kiln.

The only missing element of the kiln is the upper chamber in which pots were stacked for firing. The absence of any trace of either a permanent foundation for its walls or a central support for its roof suggests that it was probably a temporary structure of clay built around the stacked pottery. A dome would have been difficult to build without a supporting column and it would have been subject to cracking under the influence of the intense heat from the kiln. It is likely, therefore, that the pottery packed on top of the roof of the firing chamber was surrounded by a convex wall of clay, which served to

ered its floor to a depth of about 3 cm., as a courtyard in which pots were fashioned (Fig. 115). This yellow clay also coated the sides of the low walls that defined the area. The only remaining facility of the potter's workshop

117. Amphora found in the courtyard beside Kiln G

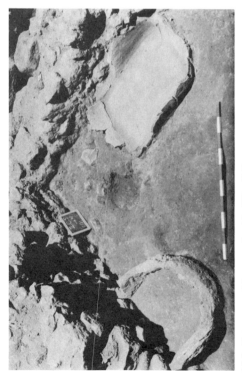

116. Pottery-working area beside Kiln C-D

divert the heat from the kiln into the stacks of pottery. The opening at the top would have served both as a chimney and as a means of access for closing the large flues around the top perimeter of the firing chamber.

An indication of the date for the use of the Kiln G complex was provided by the C-14 analysis of charred wood associated with it. When the floor of Room 74 was re-

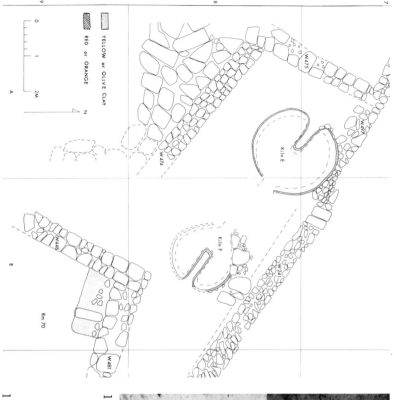

YELLOW or OLIVE CLAY

RED or ORANGE

W 475

W 497

Kiln E

W 474

W 448

W 241

Kiln F

W 241

Rm 70

W 481

0   1   2M

N

A

B

118. Plans of Kilns E and F

119. Cemented channel or basin for water

face of the tops of the remaining walls of the courtyard suggests that they stand at their original height and that they are in fact nothing more than retainers to separate the pottery working area of Room 70 from the court of the kilns.

In addition to the kilns and contiguous workrooms for fabricating and drying the vessels, there was a third essential element in the installations for making pottery: a tank for levigating clay. Best preserved of several of these settling basins is one that was given the designation of Room 58, even though it was completely surrounded by walls without entranceways, and could only have been a closed basin below the level of the surrounding area. Further evidence that it had served as a tank for washing and storing clay was provided by a coating of cement on the inside faces of its four walls and a deposit of ca. 0.30 m. of sandy clay mixed with stones on its floor. Although the walls were plastered, the floor was not. Apparently the water added to the clay in the process of levigation was allowed to seep out slowly through the floor of the tank. The source for the water used in washing the clay could not be traced because of disturbance of the surrounding area in subsequent building operations, but the remains of a cemented channel were found some 5 m. to the south. Water had been readily available in the immediate vicinity (Fig. 119).

moved, a post hole, .45 m. deep, was discovered to the north of wall 489. The lower part of the post was found in it. When this material was analyzed in the C-14 laboratory of the University Museum's Applied Science Center for Archaeology, it was found to have a date of 1290 ±52 B.C. (5730 half-life with M.I.T.-MASCA correction). Since the post was probably the support for a temporary shelter erected in the courtyard when it was in operation, it would seem likely that Kiln G is to be dated to somewhere within the thirteenth century B.C.

When Kiln G and its adjacent workroom fell into disuse, its stoking room was filled in, the entire area was leveled off, except for the terrace wall (wall 448) which had separated the two levels, and two new kilns were constructed (Fig. 118). Only the lower parts of the firing chambers of Kilns E and F remain. Although Kiln E is of approximately the same size as the earlier Kiln G, its shape is circular rather than oval. To the southeast a second kiln (F), slightly smaller, was built on a similar rounded plan. Both are located within the same courtyard and had been fired from the same level.

Associated with these two kilns is a courtyard, Room 70. Yellow clay covered its floor and the inside faces of its walls. A platform of clay at its northwestern corner served as a step to provide easy access to the room from the courtyard where the kilns are located. The finished sur-

Samples of the types of wares produced by the genera-tions of potters at Sarepta was provided by a number of deposits of sherds from discarded vessels which had mis-fired. These cracked, blistered, and warped vessels unfit for use were tossed on a pile of "wasters" by the potter as he unloaded the kiln after firing. Unfortunately the sev-eral waster deposits had generally been moved from their original positions beside the kilns from which they had come and had been used elsewhere as filling in the con-struction of buildings of a later period. Yet these large de-posits of sherds—the largest was in II-B-7, level 4, and contained 235 baskets—constituted a valuable index to the production of the several periods of fabrication and evidenced the magnitude of the ceramic industry at Sarepta.

While it is possible that the potters produced wares for export, either for sale elsewhere or for containing local products such as wine and oil shipped abroad, it is likely that the domestic market for ceramic ware in a large city could easily have absorbed a considerable production. Foods were stored and later cooked in pottery vessels. In addition to the common amphora with two handles there was the large pithos, which could be implanted more or less permanently in the ground for bulk storage. Lamps were made of pottery, as were wall brackets, which were pierced to hang on a peg driven into the wall and equipped

with a shelf that protruded at the bottom to hold an oil lamp. Large tubs, some of them fitted with a drain at the base, served industrial purposes such as dyeing cloth or mixing slip to be applied to the surface of dishes or jugs (Fig. 120). Figurines of animals and humans came to serve other than utilitarian purposes; incense stands and model houses and shrines were religious or ornamental in function. Considering the many uses to which objects of fired clay were put, it is no wonder that the potter's quarter was extensive.

In the development of ceramic technology, which is documented in the ancient Near East from as far back as the second half of the fifth millennium B.C., the kilns at Sarepta can be identified with a particular stage. Gilbert Delacroix and Jean-Louis Huot have recently studied the types of kilns dating from the fifth millennium down to the time of Alexander.[1] Throughout this long range of time, kilns of two types have been constructed: those built on the surface and those with a firing chamber below ground. Of the former the simplest is an oven that contained both the combustible fuel and the pottery to be fired. To achieve a more even distribution of heat the pots were placed on an elevated platform and the fuel was burned immediately below or in a chamber slightly to the side. The second general class of kilns consisted of those which had

[1] Syria, 49, 1972, pp. 35-95.

potteries the motor-driven wheel has replaced the hand- or kick-wheel and oil is used for fuel in place of brush and wood. However, at the village of Beit Shehab, 30 km. northeast of Beirut, a more primitive technology has survived and the methods of fabrication and firing have been described by Vronwy Hankey.[2] Deep yellow clay dug from nearby terraces is levigated from four to five months in a series of settling beds and then stored in a cellar adjoining the potter's workroom. When jars have been formed—base and shoulder are thrown on a wheel but the body is built up from ropes of clay—they are stored indoors for several weeks until they are white dry. Usually firing takes place three times during the manufacturing season, which extends from May to late September.

After the pots are loaded in the kiln a wood fire is kept burning in the firing chamber for eight days at a maximum temperature of about 800 degrees centigrade. The kiln is allowed to cool gradually for 24 hours and then emptied of its contents. Breakage and spoiling during the firing process are estimated at a rate of about three percent of the total number of vessels placed in the kiln.

The principal difference between the equipment used at Beit Shehab and that found at Sarepta is in the construction of the kiln. At the present-day site the kiln consists of two horizontal chambers, which have the advantage

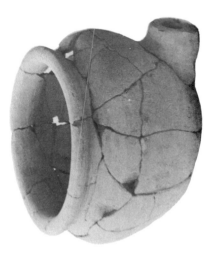

120. Terracotta tub with drainage spout at the bottom

a firing box below the surface. This construction had the advantage of added insulation for the walls of the firing chamber to conserve the heat from the fire, and a more adequate control of the draft of air for combustion could be maintained. The Sarepta kilns belonged to the second stage in this scheme of technological development.

The ancient craft of pottery making is practiced today at a number of places in the Lebanon, although in most

[2] *Palestine Exploration Quarterly*, 100, 1968, pp. 27-32.

of allowing the horizontal as well as a vertical circulation of the hot gasses from the fire. This arrangement allows a more even distribution of heat throughout the area in which the vessels are stacked, and the draft is easier to control. With this one exception the methods of pottery making at Beit Shebab are apparently the same as those which were employed at Sarepta in the Late Bronze and Iron Ages. Surely the fuel was wood and the careful attention of the potter day and night for approximately a week was essential then as now.

A deposit of crushed *murex* shells in a refuse pit of the industrial area evidenced the production of a purple dye for which the Phoenicians were famous. It was made by a process which has long been known from Classical sources and recently duplicated by scientists. Pliny has described in his *Natural History* the procedure for crushing the shell of this mollusk and extracting a colorless mucus from a gland found in its body to make a distinctive purple dye, which, he said, had "the color of congealed blood, blackish at first glance but gleaming when held up to the light."[3]

Following the directions given by Pliny and other Classical writers, F. and M. Bruin and F. W. Heineken, scientists at the American University of Beirut, produced in 1961 a small sample of the famous "royal purple" from living specimens of the famous *murex trunculus* taken from the Mediterranean by divers.[4] After the shells had been broken with a hammer, the bodies were removed and placed in a pan of salt water, where they were allowed to remain for forty-eight hours. The decaying bodies were then skimmed off and the remaining dark violet liquid was boiled for half an hour to precipitate the pure purple dye. When the product was tested by electron-spin-resonance spectroscopy its molecular patterns were found to be identical to those of the German synthetic bluish-violet dye known as 6,6'-dibromo-indigo. The yield was extremely small, averaging about .1 milligram per mollusk. Bruin estimated that one gram of pure dye was roughly equivalent in value to ten to twenty grams of gold. There was good reason for the widely used designation "royal" purple.

The deposit of crushed *murex* shells was found in a pit, measuring 1 by .50 m., cut to a depth of .20 m. into the floor of the room from which Kiln G was fired (Fig.

---

[3] 9, 62, 135.

[4] F. Bruin, "Royal Purple and the Dye Industries of the Mycenaeans and Phoenicians," *Sociétés et compagnies de commerce en orient et dans l'Océan Indien, Actes du huitième colloque international d'histoire maritime* (Beyrouth 5-10 Septembre, 1966), Michel Mollat, ed., pp. 73-90; Glenn T. Seaborg, "Science and the Humanities: A New Level of Symbiosis," *Science*, 144, 1964, pp. 1201-2.

121. Crushed shell of *murex*

122. Complete shell from a *murex trunculus*

121). The quantity collected from the disposal pit and from the surface of the floor was sufficient to fill ten of the standard rubber baskets used in the excavation. Among the fragments were a few whole specimens, one of which was eventually identified by the Academy of Natural Sciences of Philadelphia as *murex trunculus* (Fig. 122).

The site where the shells had been crushed and the dye extracted was not located; but since the refuse pit was less than four meters away from the southern limit of the excavated area, it is quite possible that the workshop may eventually be identified. Two large jars, found within the same level as that to which Kiln G belonged, had a distinctive feature that could have been useful in the production of dye (Fig. 120). A liquid could be contained in the jar by plugging the large spout at the base; by removing the plug the liquid could be drained completely while the jar remained in place. The container could also have provided a means for separating a liquid from lighter material which floated on the top.

Although the actual evidence for the working of metal within the industrial area is scant, when it is combined with that found in Sounding Y (see p. 78) there are indications that metal objects were cast at Sarepta. Amorphous pieces of metal and bits of slag were found in various strata, and a rim sherd from a crucible, which had measured about 27 cm. in diameter, appeared in the balk that separated squares II-B-9 and II-C-9. Slag coated its inside surface; and the slag, in turn, was covered by a thin layer of green material, which was obviously an oxide of the copper which the crucible contained. Since there were no remains of a furnace in which this crucible might have been used, one must suppose that it either lies in a part of the city that is as yet unexplored or was destroyed in one of the rebuildings of the area.

A mold for jewelry evidenced both the method employed in casting and the forms of the pieces produced. The mold consists of a flat piece of dark green steatite, measuring 5.6 cm. wide, 5.9 cm. long, and 1.8 cm. thick (Fig. 123). Both sides are carved with matrices in which articles of jewelry were cast from the molten metal introduced through funnels cut into the edges of the mold.

The steatite block is but one element of a closed mold. To have been serviceable the matrices carved on each side would have had exact duplicates (cut in mirror images, of course) cut into another block of steatite. When the elements of the closed mold were aligned with dowels (one hole for a dowel remains), clamped together and supported in a bed of sand so that the pour-channels were upright, the molten metal was poured.

The original mold may have consisted of either two or three pieces. The element which has survived could have

been used with one additional block of steatite carved on both sides with mirror images of the matrices. When the matching faces had been clamped together and the casts made, the stones could have been reversed and the matrices of the opposing sides utilized. However, it is possible that the preserved element is the middle part of a three-element mold. With two matrices clamped to it, one pouring of the metal would have produced all the forms in one operation.

The forms of the objects which were cast are varied. On one side there appear matrices for a spacer, an elongated bead, a lunate pendant or earring, a finger ring and a bifurcated wirelike object; on the other, a trinket in the shape of a keyhole, and spherical beads. In addition to the

123. The two sides of a jewelry mold

grooves cut in the mold as channels for the molten metal there appear deeper grooves which bisect the matrices for the twenty beads. Obviously these were designed to hold pins of some disposable material, such as wood, to serve as a core for producing the holes in the beads. A similar groove has been provided to cast the holes for the lunate pendant, long bead, and spacer on the other side of the mold.

The latest industrial use of Sounding X was in the post-Phoenician times of the Hellenistic and Roman occupations. An elaborate olive press was installed in II-C/D-9 (Fig. 124). The largest element of the installation is a crushing basin, 1.60 m. in diameter, hewn from a single stone (A). The heavy stone roller which crushed the olives was missing, but a circular groove in which it had been turned was apparent. On the floor around the basin there was a well-worn path beaten down by the worker, or workers, who had operated the crusher by rotating the crushing wheel.

Eighty centimeters to the east stands the base of the press, a large circular stone with a low rim to contain the olive pulp produced in the crushing process (B). Here the crushed, ripe olives had been placed and pressure had

124. Olive press: crusher, press, catch basin, and drum

been applied from above to squeeze out the oil, which was allowed to flow through a groove in the rim of the pressing stone into a stone container adjacent to it. The oil vat, hewn from a solid drum of stone, had a capacity of 37½ gallons (C). To the south, but at a lower level, a cement-lined tank, 1.20 by 1.58 m., provided a storage facility, probably for the olive pits and pulp, which could be swept conveniently into it from the press (D).

These elements of the press complex seemed to have obvious functions. However, another object within the well-defined area of the press is more difficult to interpret. It is a large column drum, .70 m. in diameter and .95 m. high, and weighing about 800 kilograms (E). It could have served as a weight for applying pressure to the pressing stone. Its top had been carefully cut so as to provide a socket for a wooden upright with a diameter of approximately .20 m. Lateral and inverted wedge-shaped cuttings at the sides of the socket provided the means for securing the element. If the stone had been revolved, the wooden

upright would also have turned with it. Inverted wedges attached to the wooden upright would have made it possible to lift the stone drum by the wooden attachment.

One can only speculate as to how the press functioned. The most plausible explanation is that pressure was applied to the crushed olives lying in the pressing basin at the fulcrum of a horizontal beam, which had one end set firmly into a wall. If the other end had been attached to the stone drum by means of a screw, pressure could have been applied to the pressing basin in the middle by turning the stone drum. But since we have no evidence for the use of the threaded screw at this or contemporary sites, the function of the large drum is far from certain.

Although only a relatively small area within the city of Sarepta has been explored, the specialized use of Sounding X for industrial enterprises and the general absence of domestic quarters in the area of the kilns and workshops suggest that a kind of rudimentary zoning was employed in the organization of urban life.

VIII

The Shrine of Tanit-Ashtart

WHAT is known about the religion of the Phoenicians during the heyday of their commercial and colonial enterprises has been derived principally from inscriptions and from tantalizing details concerning their religious rites as presented in biblical and classical sources. The names of the gods and goddesses are well known from monuments erected to them in the homeland and abroad. Punic inscriptions found at Marseilles and at Carthage list the tariff of payments to be made to the priest for sacrifices ($ANET^3$, 656-57). Occasionally outsiders recorded details of the cult which impressed them. An Israelite writer described the futile attempts of Phoenician prophets of Baal to gain the attention of their god by dancing and cutting themselves with swords and lances "till the blood gushed out upon them" (I Kings 18:28). Lucian, writing in the second century A.D., said he witnessed at Byblos such religious rites as lamentations, shaving the hair from the head, and women offering themselves for prostitution— practices which could have reached back to Phoenician times.[1] These and other writings serve to document the character of Phoenician cultic practices.

[1] *De Dea Syria*, 6.

The archaeological remains, however, of a shrine or temple where Phoenicians worshiped their gods in the homeland had not been known until the discovery of the shrine of Tanit-Ashtart at Sarepta in 1972. Temples from an earlier period than the Iron Age had been found at Byblos; and the temple of Eshmun, near Sidon, had provided a picture of the cult of the healing god as it was practiced in the sixth century and later. But for the period of the Phoenician prominence, from about 1200 to 600 B.C., no actual remains of a religious structure had come to light.

The shrine at Sarepta is built on the edge of the mound, overlooking the harbor, which lies some 50 m. to the north (A-4 and B-4 of the grid in Fig. 39); the industrial area of the city is located directly to the south and is separated from the shrine by a narrow street. The long axis of the rectangular structure is orientated east-west and measures 6.40 m.; the average width of the building is 2.56 m., but at the east end it is .32 m. wider than it is at the west, a discrepancy which was occasioned by the builder's use of earlier walls as foundations (Fig. 125). The shrine was provided with slightly more than 16 sq. m. of floor space. A street runs beside the south wall (471), turns to the

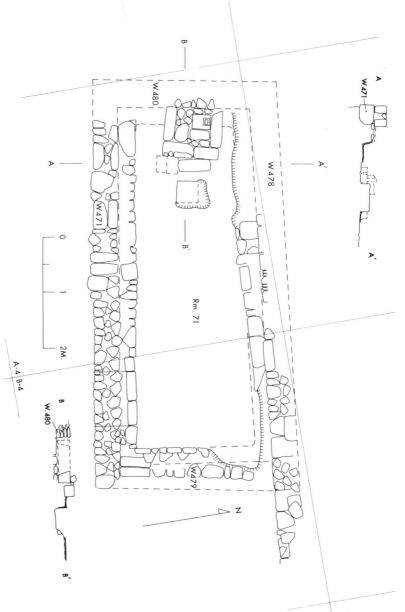

125. Plan of the shrine in II-A/B-4

left at the corner to follow the shrine's east wall (479) to its end, and then makes a turn eastward to connect with a principal entrance into the city from the port to the north.

The building had been constructed with more than usual care. Foundations for its walls are deep. To judge from the one course of the superstructure that remains (Fig. 126), the walls are built with well-cut sandstone blocks set in the attractive header-and-stretcher pattern. The floor, unlike the usual clay floors found in the industrial and residential areas, is a thick layer of hard, gray cement, averaging about .10 m. in thickness, laid over a foundation of pebbles and sand. The surface is finished off smoothly.

The shrine had an entrance from the street. During the last period of its use there appears to have been a doorway at the north end of the east wall; although the wall is missing, an entrance is indicated by the extension of the cement floor beyond the inside line of the wall. Originally, however, the entrance had been around the corner, at the east end of the south wall. In the excavation of the sloping street that flanked the south wall we were able to see a practical reason for this minor architectural change in the sanctuary's plan. The street sloped downward to the east. Rain water had coursed down this passageway—there were no gutters—bearing with it pebbles and silt that raised the

126. The shrine as seen from the east

level of the surface of the street. Eventually, as the street reached the level of the shrine's threshold, water from a downpour would have threatened to flood the room. Probably it was then that the doorway was blocked, the bench extended across the open space of the first entrance, and a new doorway cut in the east wall, where the adjacent street was lower. Winter rains could no longer menace the shrine.

It was not until two years after the shrine room had been cleared that a discovery made in the room to the north provided some indirect evidence for yet another entrance into the shrine (Fig. 127). Lying on the floor of the room to the north were some votive objects of the same type as those found within the shrine itself. In the earlier season we had assumed that the break in the west end of the north wall (478) was due to the work of stone looters and that originally it had extended along the entire length of the shrine room. But when votive objects were found beyond the line of the hypothetical wall it seemed probable that there had been a doorway through which these objects had been carried from the shrine. If this hypothesis is correct, then it is possible that the adjacent room may have served as the living quarters for the shrine's custodian or priest and that the doorway provided convenient access for the religious functionaries.

Three distinctive features built into the room attest its use as a shrine or chapel. Although these elements of cultic

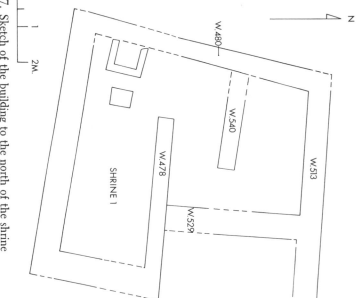

127. Sketch of the building to the north of the shrine

furniture are unique for Phoenicia proper, parallels for each of them have been found in structures which have been identified as temples at Canaanite sites in neighboring Palestine or at colonies established by the Phoenicians. Added support for the cultic interpretation of one feature of the shrine is provided, as we shall see, by a representation of the Phoenician temple at Byblos found on the obverse of a coin of the Roman period.

Benches, averaging ca. .20 m. in height and varying in width from .30 to .40 m., are evidenced along each of the room's four walls. Built of fieldstones set in mortar, these projections from the walls had been covered with cement so as to provide a smooth upper surface. The best preserved of these benches is the segment along the south wall of the building (wall 471); from fragments of a similar construction on the other walls it is clear that the benches had encircled the room except for the entranceways and the segment of the west wall against which the table had been built.

This feature of temple furniture has long been known. Benches around the walls of cultic buildings have been discovered over the last fifty years at numerous sites in Palestine. The three Late Bronze Age temples at Lachish, in southern Judah, were all equipped with them; so were the temples of the same period found at Beth-shan in the north. Recently Yigael Yadin found three temples of the

128. Offering table and socket for standing pillar

Late Bronze Age at Hazor; each exhibited this architectural feature. The traditional style did not die out easily but was maintained well into the succeeding centuries of the Iron Age, as shrines and temples at Beth-shan, Arad, Lachish and Tell Qasile testify.

Benches appear as the hallmark of cultic architecture not only on the mainland but on Cyprus as well. At Enkomi Claude Schaeffer found that the walls of the twelfth-century "Sanctuaire du dieu au lingot" were flanked by benches; and even as late as the sixth-fifth century the builders of the Kition temple had continued the tradition.

The function of the so-called benches has been debated. The prevailing opinion is that they were not for seating, as the term might imply, but that they served to hold offerings brought to the temple by the worshipers. Yet there was no evidence at Sarepta to support this interpretation. As we shall see later, all the votive objects left within the shrine were found concentrated in the area at the west end of the room; none was discovered along the benches that lined the other walls.

The second distinctive feature with which the room was equipped is a table, measuring 1.02 by .92 m., built against the west wall (Fig. 128). Its top had been robbed, but a course of ashlar blocks protruding above the level of the floor preserved its plan. The three exposed sides of the table had been faced with slabs of gypsum; a portion of one of them remained in place on the east side and extended for .20 m. above the remaining stone structure behind it. How high the table stood originally it is impossible to say, but the presence of a low step in front of the structure would suggest that the top was considerably higher than the remaining stones and gypsum facing. If the step had served to elevate a functionary or worshiper, as would seem reasonable, so that he had convenient access to the top of the table, the structure may have been built to as much as a meter and a half above the level of the floor.

A large cache of votive objects, which we shall describe later, found in the area in front of and beside the table provides evidence for its function. Most likely the table served as an altar on which worshipers placed gifts brought to the shrine and presented to the deity. A comparable structure has been discovered at Kition on Cyprus, where a Phoenician temple belonging to the period extending from about 600 to 450 B.C. has been found by V. Karageorghis.2 There the altar is 1.55 m. square and is faced on its four sides with slabs of gypsum. From this striking parallel and the presence of votive objects around it, there can be little doubt that our altar served as the focal point of the shrine, the place where offerings were placed in devotion to the god.

2 F. Barreca et al., L'espansione fenicia nel Mediterraneo, 1971, pp. 171-72.

130. The stone after removal of cover

129. Worked stone found in the offering table, before removal of cover

While the use to which the offering table had been put seemed obvious, a device which had been fashioned from a block of sandstone and carefully placed in the filling of the table could not be easily explained (Figs. 129 and 130). The stone, measuring 28 by 32 by 20 cm., has a basin, 4 cm. deep, cut into its upper face. At the bottom of this depression is a drain which leads toward the center of the block; two channels emerge, one at the short side and another at the long side of the stone. The connection between the drain for the basin on top and the two outlets was discovered only by chance when the object was being measured and sketched for publication a year after it had been taken from the offering table.

The device was more intricate than we had first supposed. In addition to the basin cut into the face of the block there was detected a carefully trimmed slab of stone which had been fitted over a cylindrical cutting. The slab had been cemented over so that it was impossible to detect its presence from above. It was in this concealed cylindrical chamber that the drain from the basin met the two channels leading to the sides of the stone. If one channel was plugged at its outlet a liquid would have drained from the other. From the careful fitting of the stone cover and the cement which had covered the joins it seemed probable that the intention had been to conceal this connection between the basin and the two channels through which a

liquid would drain from one or the other of the channels at the side.

It is, of course, possible that this well-fashioned block, with its basin and channels, served some practical purpose in domestic life, but its presence within the altar of the shrine—it appeared to have been carefully placed with basin upward at the northwest corner of the table—makes it likely that it had had some previous cultic use. If indeed it was a sacred relic, then the offering table in which it was built would have taken on the added sanctity of a cultic object which had been used in a more ancient rite. The disguise of the connection between the channels may have served to produce a marvel that impressed the devotees of the cult. However, its use remains a puzzle.

The third feature with which the shrine had been equipped was a pillar set firmly in the cement floor immediately in front of the offering table (Fig. 128). This sacred object had been pried loose from its setting and carried away, but its socket remained to indicate its position and two of its dimensions. The break in the cement floor appears about .20 m. to the east of the step before the table and measures about .50 by .60 m. The depression was filled to a depth of .20 m. with yellow clay and stone chips; below, a thin layer of dark carbonized material covered the filling for the cement floor. The edges of the socket on the north and east sides are ragged and broken; but those to the west and south are preserved with a smooth face for a distance of .40 m. in each direction. Obviously the object, whose base had been .40 by .40 m., had been pried loose to the northeast by pressure which had broken the cement around its base on those two sides. One would judge that the stone must have had a con-

siderable height—possibly as much as one meter—to have provided leverage sufficient to destroy the cement, .13 to .19 m. thick, on the north and east sides in the process of removal. From the central position which this pillar occupied one can conclude that it was an important feature in the arrangement of the cultic furniture.

Standing stones were a characteristic feature of religious shrines of the Canaanite cult, which was closely related to the Phoenician. Memorable is the iconoclasm practiced by the adherents of the rival religion of Yahweh, who broke the pillars (*maṣṣeboth*) and cut down the wooden post (*'asherah*) (II Kings 18:4) in the days of Hezekiah, king of Judah. Recently the excavations at Hazor in northern Palestine have laid bare a Canaanite shrine of the thirteenth century B.C., in which standing stones are the accompaniment of the offering table (*ANEP*² 871). A parallel geographically closer to the standing stone at Sarepta is the illustration of the temple at Byblos found on the reverse of a coin of the third century A.D. Here the central feature of an elaborate temple is a large conical stone, or baetyl (Fig. 131).

Whether the standing pillar was stone or wood it is impossible to tell, although the dark carbonized material, mentioned above, found at the bottom of the socket would suggest the latter. A further possibility is that the object which stood before the offering table was a horned incense altar made of stone, of the type found at Megiddo, which has a square base, but of slightly smaller dimensions.[3]

The room of the shrine is too small to have been used for public ceremonies; a score of people would have filled it. Its primary function would seem to have been to contain the gifts brought to the deity whose shrine it was. Although there is no evidence for either the presence or absence of windows, twelve saucer lamps, each of which have traces of carbon around the pinched spout, lay nestled on the step before the offering table. The presence of these lamps makes possible the reconstruction of an eerie room in which oil lamps burning on the offering table produced an effect of mystery. Some light would have filtered in from the one-meter-wide opening from the street, but little would have been available from the carefully shielded doorway leading to the room to the north.

For some reason, impossible to establish from the material evidence, the small chapel was later replaced by a larger one. The lines for the south and west walls of the earlier building were preserved, probably because of the street that bordered those sides; the walls on the other two sides were moved outward from the lines of the earlier shrine so as to enlarge considerably the area of the room. Over a filling of yellow clay a layer of reddish cement was laid and this in turn was topped with a slightly thinner layer of gray cement to provide a floor, which was about .40 m. above that of the earlier shrine. It is this slab of cement, preserved in part, which provides what we have of the general plan of the room. All of its stone walls had been robbed, but the trenches of the looters could be detected. Such cultic furniture as benches, table, and baetyl, which had characterized the earlier building, was not duplicated as far as could be determined from the portions of the floor that had survived the destruction wrought by later builders who cut it when digging their foundations. Yet, the presence of clay figurines of the seated mother type in the debris which filled the building would suggest that its function, like that of its predecessor, had been cultic.

The identification of the small room as a religious shrine—an identification made because of the distinctive features of benches, offering table, and the socket for a baetyl—was strengthened by the discovery of a collection of more than two hundred votive objects. They came, for the most part, from the filling within and on top of the offering table, from the socket for the standing pillar, from the floor of the room, and from the robbers' trench cut for removing the stones from the west end of the north wall of the building. All the objects came from the west end of the room and most lay within the immediate vicinity of

[3] H. G. May, *Material Remains of the Megiddo Cult*, 1935, pl. 12, no. 2982.

the offering table. Obviously this collection of trinkets came from the *favissa*, the repository of gifts brought to the sacred place as offerings to the deity.

The objects from the cache fell into several broad categories: figurines, carved pieces of ivory, amulets in human and animal form as well as in the form of the Egyptian "Eye of Horus," cosmetic equipment, beads, a cultic mask, gaming pieces, and lamps. Most of the objects are made from such common and easily available materials as potter's clay, faience, stone (for some of the beads); four pieces of ivory and one alabaster vessel appear; but noticeably absent are such expensive materials as gold and silver. The impression given is that these are the kinds of votive objects which the poor, rather than the rich, would have presented.

Most striking is the presence of such a large number of Egyptian objects in a Phoenician shrine. Amulets representing the dwarf Bes (Fig. 132), Ptah, Bastet (Fig. 133), the cat, Horus (Fig. 134), and the sow (Fig. 135); there are 14 examples of the *wajet* or "Eye of Horus" (Fig. 136). These faience amulets, indistinguishable from similar examples found in Egypt, are probably trade items imported from Egypt. The Phoenician peasants of Sarepta, if indeed they knew what Egyptian gods were represented in these trinkets, apparently did not consider it inappropriate to make use of them as offerings in their own cult.

131. Standing pillar within the temple at Byblos, on the reverse of a coin from the third century A.D.

133. Amulet of a cat-headed human figure

132. Faience amulet of the Egyptian god Bes

134. The Egyptian god Horus as a child

There is evidence, however, that the local cult was syncretistic, at least in its iconography. The mixing of motifs is particularly apparent in the fragmentary clay throne flanked by two sphinxes (Fig. 137, center). Fashioned from clay, it had been broken even before it had been buried in the debris and important details lost. Fortunately, its original form could be reconstructed on the basis of other examples, which have been found in three widely scattered places, of this representation of a figure seated on a throne.

The most prominent sphinx throne is that depicted on the sarcophagus of Ahiram, King of Byblos (see Chapter II). From a slightly earlier period an ivory plaque found at the Palestinian site of Megiddo has a representation of a prince sitting on a sphinx throne and receiving offerings and tribute brought to him by his courtiers. And even farther afield, in Galera, Spain, there has been found a female figure ("Astarte") seated on a throne supported by two winged sphinxes, a representation which has been thought by Spanish archaeologists to be Phoenician in origin.

The Sarepta figure is a relatively crude example of this well-known motif. The craftsman responsible for it made use of elements which are unmistakably Egyptian: the high crown, painted blue, on the sphinx's head and the rectangular false beard under the chin. The long pendant

135. The sow represented on a faience amulet

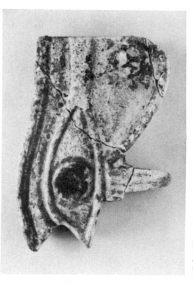

136. The "Eye of Horus"

137. Terracotta figurines from the shrine: figure with a drum (left), the sphinx throne (center), and the woman with a dove (right)

138. Head from the sphinx throne

139. Woman's head carved from ivory

locks at the side of the neck are more in the style of Syrian representations. This terracotta figure is probably a local product produced by a Phoenician craftsman who was strongly influenced by Egyptian styles.

Although only the torso of the enthroned figure and a part of the skirt remain, it is clear that the feet had been attached to the underside of the seat. They had probably rested on a footstool as did the feet of King Ahiram. Whether the enthroned figure was a man, as on the Byblos sarcophagus and the Megiddo ivory, or a woman, as represented on the Galera figure, it is impossible to say.

The damaged piece with only one head of the sphinx throne remaining was found in the 1972 season of excavation. Two years later the other head was found when the area just north of the north wall of the shrine was excavated (Fig. 138). This discovery of a missing piece of the object served to demonstrate that the hoard of cultic objects extended to the north and that there had been an entrance into the shrine from the room adjoining it at the north.

Although Phoenician ivories have long been known from sites in Assyria (Nimrud and Khorsabad), Syria (Arslan Tash), and Palestine (Samaria), practically no examples had come from the Phoenician coastal cities themselves. One of the two pieces of carved ivory found in the shrine depicts the head of a woman, wearing a heavy wig of Egyptian type which covers half of the forehead and extends downward at the sides to the level of the shoulders (Fig. 139). At first glance the plaque seemed identical to heads which have been found at Samaria and at Nimrud and known as the "woman at the window." Our ivory depicts the same half-smiling face of a woman and has the uraeus symbol just above the forehead. However, one feature of the Sarepta plaque sets it apart from the long known examples: a collar with three strands of lotus decoration. This feature of the carving appears on the head of a sphinx found at Khorsabad carved from a single piece of ivory, which had probably been used as an inlay for wooden furniture. Evidently sphinxes in ivory as well as in clay had been fashioned and used at Sarepta.

Among the votive objects found in the shrine the largest class of objects (with the exception of beads) was that of terracotta figurines. While animals fashioned from clay were found in other areas of the excavation, the figurines taken from the shrine were all representations of human beings. And whenever enough of the figurine was preserved to make possible the identification of the sex, the figure bore female characteristics. Not only were there no male figurines of clay but there was a noticeable lack of such votive gifts as weapons, which one would expect from men. The clear impression from inventory of votive offerings from the favissa is that they had been presented by women or that they were offerings which were considered appropriate for a goddess.

The best preserved of the terracotta figurines is that of a woman holding a stylized bird in her arms (Fig. 137, right). Red paint decorates the ears and lips and a broad vertical stripe, 3 cm. wide, appears running down the front of the bell-shaped body. The face had been pressed in a mold and the head was attached by a dowel to the body, which had been fashioned on a wheel. The long locks of hair had been made by hand and attached to the sides of the head and shoulders. Two other heads from the same type of figurine attested the popularity of this style of representation.

Another figure, of which a number of fragments were found, is that of a seated woman playing a hand drum or tambourine (Fig. 137, left). She wears a long robe on which the vertical borders are clearly indicated on the left side by a line in the clay and four lines of paint, two red and two black. A similar treatment (although the paint is faded) appears on the right side as well. The belly protrudes slightly and the navel is represented. The player held a tambourine with the left hand; the right hand is missing. She sat on a stool, of which little survives.

The third general type of figurine is that of the seated pregnant woman (Fig. 140); the popularity of this type, attested by many fragments from other models, seems to have been reached at the time of the building of the second shrine above the remains of the first. The woman wears a long garment and is seated on a stool. The neck of the garment is decorated with three horizontal bands or stripes of red paint. Either from the edge of the garment or from a slot in it the right hand protrudes and rests over the distended abdomen. The slightly bowed head wears a head-dress or wig with heavy locks that hang at either side of the face to a line just below the shoulders. Traces of red paint that once decorated the ears remain. The intention seems clear: a chaste representation of a woman awaiting patiently the time of parturition. Unlike the woman hold-ing the stylized bird, this figurine is widely attested in Phoenicia, Palestine, and Cyprus.

What we have mentioned thus far are artifacts which one would expect, from their iconography and symbolism, to be found in a cultic context: amulets of Egyptian deities, the sphinx throne, the woman's head wearing the sacred uraeus, and figurines that suggest a magical or re-ligious function. Yet mixed with these specifically cultic objects are others which are known to have been used in everyday life as articles of personal adornment and groom-ing. Almost half of the inventory of the contents of the *favissa* consisted of beads. While 96 beads is not a large number to have been recovered, the diversity of materials from which they were made—faience, frit, carnelian, glass, shell, and bone—and the variety of shapes found among them—annular, flat with reticulation, cylindrical, barrel-shaped, lenticular, and gadrooned—suggest that this assort-ment is only a sample from many strings of beads, each pre-sumably more or less homogeneous as to material and shape. In addition to the beads there was found an alabaster con-

140. Figurine of a seated, pregnant woman

tainer for *kohl* or eye-paint (Fig. 67) and the faience top of a round box. Both of these objects are familiar cosmetic equipment used by women.

The range and diversity of the gifts remaining in the shrine can best be seen from the following inventory of catalogued objects: Terracotta shrine fragment, mask, lid for cosmetic box, alabaster *kohl* jar, incense stand, sphinx throne, Shawabti figure, Horus figure, baboon figure, 6 carved ivory pieces, 14 playing pieces, 14 lamps, 33 amulets, 36 figurines in terracotta, 96 beads, and 4 miscellaneous fragments.

This collection of votive objects is sufficiently large to permit some generalizations about the kinds of gifts which were presented to the deity. How restricted the assemblage of items is can be seen when it is compared with two groups of artifacts from other contexts. The first is what remains of the material culture in the industrial and domestic areas of the city, an assemblage which consists principally of bowls, jugs, jars, cooking pots, tools, and weapons. All of these artifacts are noticeably absent in the *favissa* of the shrine. Such utilitarian objects in common use day after day in the life of the city were apparently not considered appropriate for gifts to the deity of the shrine. A comparison may also be made with the repertoire of objects generally placed in burials. While the cemetery of

the Iron Age at Sarepta has not yet been discovered, we do have evidence of burial practices from the preceding period. The evidence found in five burials at Sarepta is of grave goods which consist primarily of ceramic dishes and containers and an occasional bead or finger ring.

When this assortment of gifts is set alongside these two groups of utilitarian artifacts, the criteria of selection are more apparent. The offerings consisted largely of trinkets of a personal nature, such as amulets, beads, cosmetic equipment, or of figurines and statuettes of musicians, the pregnant woman, and an enthroned personage. Whether this selection of gifts reflects what was considered of value to the donor or what was thought to be desirable to the divine recipient, it is difficult to say. Although lamps and playing pieces could be associated with either men or women, the presence in the collection of offerings of such a large number of female figurines and so many articles of personal adornment usually associated with women would suggest that the shrine was frequented principally by women or that the recipient of the gifts was a goddess, for whom such gifts were appropriate.

With over two hundred votive objects available for study it seemed at the conclusion of the excavation that dates for the use of the shrine could be determined easily by comparisons with similar dated material from other excavated sites. It soon became apparent, however, that many of the distinctive objects which might have been useful for dating the cache, such as the Egyptian amulets, had been manufactured and sold for centuries with no appreciable changes in style. And, if an amulet could have been assigned to a particular period of time there remained the possibility that it might have been kept within a family as an heirloom for several generations.

The earliest date which can be given with any degree of certainty to an object found within the shrine is the eighth century B.C. The ivory carving of a woman's head (Fig. 139) can be assigned on the basis of the treatment of the hair and the decoration on the collar to the general horizon of ivory work of the so-called "Layard" or Phoenician group of ivories found in Mesopotamia, which has been dated by R. D. Barnett to the eighth century.[4] There is, of course, the possibility that this piece of ivory inlay was already old—there is the noticeable wear on the nose—when it was placed in the shrine.

Another possible indicator of date is the form of the letters employed in the inscription carved on the ivory plaque described in Chapter VI. Certain of the letters display a form which were current in Phoenician writing in

[4] *Iraq*, 2, 1933, p. 185; Barnett has expressed an opinion in a communication of August 2, 1972, that the Sarepta piece is

the seventh century, but the early sixth century is not to be excluded for other forms. It is perhaps safe to date the inscription somewhere around the end of the seventh or the beginning of the sixth century.

The pieces which can serve to fix a *terminus ad quem* for the shrine's use are the figurines of the seated pregnant woman, which to judge from their appearance at other sites in Palestine, Syria, and Cyprus, belong to the fifth-fourth centuries. Since examples of this type of figurine came from the debris that filled the second or latter shrine (some examples found within the first shrine may have been intruded when the stones of the north wall were robbed for building the later structure), it would seem prudent to place the use of the later shrine in the fifth century with a possible extension into the fourth. Yet the stratigraphic contexts in which the figurines have been found at other sites is not clearly established. Thus the evidence which is available at present indicates a span for the use of the two shrines of some four centuries, extending from the eighth to the fourth centuries B.C.

The identity of the deity of the shrine was indicated by the discovery of the dedicatory plaque found within the *favissa* of the earlier shrine (Chapter VI). From the inscription—

"not later than the eighth century or early seventh century at the latest."

tion it is clear that Shillem, son of Mapaʻal, son of ʻIzai made a statue, presumably to which the plaque had been attached, for Tanit-Ashtart. Although there remains the remote possibility that this votive object had been brought from elsewhere and deposited in the shrine, it would seem more likely that the shrine in which the ivory label was found was that of Tanit-Ashtart.

This was probably only one of several shrines or temples at Sarepta. The dedication of a jar to Shadrapa and the other dedication to a god who is referred to simply as "our lord," suggest that there were other deities who were served in the city and it is possible that shrines belonging to them are also to be found.

The particular function of Tanit and Ashtart in the Phoenician-Punic religious system has long been known. Ashtart, the better known of the two goddesses, is predominantly the patroness of love and fertility, although she is also referred to as the goddess of war in certain texts. Tanit, with whom she is associated in the inscription, is better documented in the Punic world, where her name appears on thousands of stelae, many of which have been found in the context of burials of children at Carthage. Thus the associations which are known for these two goddesses, the one with fertility and the other with children converge and overlap. When these attributes which are known from literary and archaeological sources are compared with the character of the offerings found in the shrine, it would seem that we cannot be far wrong in reconstructing at Sarepta a cult where women performed their acts of devotion to the deity who provided them with the blessings of conception, successful parturition, and the nurture of children from infancy through the hazardous period of their early years.

Acknowledgment for Illustrations

William P. Anderson, 42, 43
© National Geographic Society, Robert Azzi, 114, 122, 134, 137
The Trustees of the British Museum, 13, 100, 131
EROS Data Center, 1
Gabinetto Fotografico Nazionale-Roma, 23
© National Geographic Society, Otis Imboden, 75, 111, 124
Brahim Kawkabani, 16

Ministry of National Defense, Lebanon, 2
Photo Louvre, 7
From Drawings by Edith Porada, 10, 11
Elizabeth Simpson, 12
Jack R. Sims, Jr., 31
Julian Whittlesey, 50, 54, 107, 115
Yale University, 14
All other illustrations are by expedition staff

Catalogue of Illustrated Objects

THE following catalogue of the objects presented in the illustrations provides more detailed information than has been included in the text and captions. The field number (prefixed by Sar.) will serve to identify the artifact within the large collection of excavated materials which has been deposited in the National Museum in Beirut. The grid reference, which follows the field number, is keyed to the grid plan for Area II in Fig. 39; eventually when the stratification has been worked out for Sounding X and the sections published, the references to levels will become relevant. At the present stage of study only those given for II-K-20 (the level is italicized below for easy reference) can be related to the section for that plot in Fig. 42. Colors for most of the ceramic material were registered by reference to the Munsell color charts. For these objects notation of color has been given by the number-letter system of Munsell as well as by the descriptions of color suggested in the charts.

Fig. No.

44. Sar. 3259, II-K-21, level 28 (Stratum G). Deep bowl; height, .10 m.; surface, very pale brown (10YR 7/3); matt slip painted with dark reddish brown (5YR 3/2) (exterior), 2.5YR 8.3 (interior).

45. Sar. 3241, II-K-21, level 29 (Stratum G). Storage jar; height, .56 m.; surface, pinkish white (7.5YR 8/2).

46. ——, II-L-20, level 27-1 (Stratum G). Cooking pot; diameter of rim, .26 m.; surface, red (10R 5/7).

47. Sar. 3135, II-K-21, level 28 (Stratum G). Fragment of incised terracotta plaque; width, .103 m.

48. Sar. 3174, II-L-20, level 27-3 (Stratum G). Face of

longitudinally pierced scarab, decorated with *wajet* design and other lines; length, .014 m.; green steatite.

49. ——, II-K-20, level 27-1 (Stratum F). Potter's tool cut from body sherd; width, .075 m.; surface, white (5Y 8/2).

50. Sar. 3123, II-K-20, level 27-1 (Stratum F). Rattle with holes pierced in ends and incised decoration on the cylinder; clay pellets sealed inside; length, .115 m.; surface, reddish yellow (5YR 6/6).

51. Sar. 3109, II-K-20, level 27-1 (Stratum F). Bronze weight in form of heifer; filled with lead; length; .058 m.; green patina.

52. Sar. 3046, II-K-20, level 26 (Stratum E). Conical stamp seal, pierced for suspension; height, .015 m.; blue frit.

53. Sar. 1288, II-K-21, level 7 (Stratum D). Bowl; diameter, .10 m.; surface, reddish yellow (5YR 6/7).

54. Sar. 3136, II-B-7, level 10*. Jug; height, .194 m.; surface, reddish yellow (5YR 6/7); burnished and painted with red (10R 5/6) and very dark gray (2.5YR 3/0).

55. Sar. 3001, II-L-21, level 7 (Stratum D). Storage jar; height, .58 m.; surface, pink (5YR 8/4).

56. Sar. 1359, II-K-21, Room 32, level 9 (Stratum D). Cypriot bichrome barrel juglet; height, .095 m.; surface, very pale brown (10YR 7/4) of matt slip, painted with dusky red (10R 3/2) and weak red (10R 4/3).

57. Sar. 3059, II-K-20, level 26 (Stratum E). Bowl; diameter, .17 m.; surface, medium light gray (10YR 6/1).

58. Sar. 3129, II-K-21, level 4 (?) (Stratum B). Storage jar; height, .345 m.; surface, reddish yellow (5YR 7/6).

59. Sar. 3189, II-K-21, level 31. Spindle whorl; diameter, .027 m.; polished brown/beige bone.

60. Sar. 1346, II-B-7, level 4. Clay loom weight; diameter, .07 m.; surface, salmon.

61. Sar. 1249, II-K-20, level 9. Clay loom weight; height, .08 m.; dark brown.

62. Sar. 1073, II-C-6, level 5. Bronze needle; length, .065 m.; greenish patina.

63. Sar. 2195, II-A-9, level 1b. Bronze fibula; length, .063 m.; hatched design on arms.

64. Sar. 4217, II-B-3/4, level 2. Pin with head carved in the form of a hand holding a ball. A cord or chain is represented as tied around the wrist; length, .109 m.; bone.

65. Sar. 2376, II-A-5, level 2a. Ivory pin with pomegranate carved on the head; length, .117 m.

66. Sar. 4217, II-Z-4, level 2-2. Pin with bulbous head; incisions on the body below the head; length, .10 m.; bone.

67. Sar. 3026, II-A-4, Room 71, level 3. Alabaster cosmetic container; height, .073 m.; light yellow and white, veined.

68. Sar. 4256, II-Z-2, level 2-1. Cylindrical container, decorated with incised bands. One cord-eye handle preserved near the rim; height of fragment, .067 m.; bone or ivory.

69. Sar. 1310, II-B-6, level 17. Decorated bone handle for mirror (?); preserved length, .07 m.; yellowish brown.

70. Sar. 1283, II-C/D-6/7, level 18b. Glass eye-bead;

71. Sar. 2308, II-A-8/9, Room 58, level 4. *Wajet* pendant, pierced longitudinally; width, .046 m.; soft, white material, probably frit, but possibly stone; black paint along top and on eye.

72. Sar. 2374, II-B-9, level 4. Gold earring with two links for attaching pendant; length, .027 m.; gold.

73. ———, provenience unknown. Basalt rider for a mill, with two hand-grips on top and smoothed under-surface; length, .40 m.

76. Sar. 4004, II-A-9, level not recorded. Bronze hook with barb at point and upper end flattened; height, .024 m.; green patina.

77. Sar. 3126, II-B-4, level 6-1. Head from horse figurine, with forelock; eyes and ears formed with pellets of clay; height, .061 m.; surface color, reddish yellow (5YR 6/6).

78. Sar. 4240, II-A-3, level 5-9. Human figure seated side-wise on saddle, or saddle-pack, with left hand holding the pommel; height of fragment, .068 m.; surface, light red (10R 6/8).

79. Sar. 1338, II-B-6, level 22. Head of horned animal figurine; length, .07 m.; buff terracotta with bands of dark slip or paint on neck, nose, and eyes.

80. Sar. 4219, II-C-3, level 6. Sherd incised with chariot, bowman, and reined horse; width of sherd, .10 m.; surface, red (2.5YR 5/6).

81. Sar. 1339, II-B-6, level 24. Terracotta wheel from cart or chariot; diameter, .05 m.; reddish clay.

82. Sar. 3207, II-B/C-6/7, Room 73, level 19-3. Model boat, modeled from clay, with holes in each side and at one end; length, .091 m.; yellowish red (5YR 5.5/6).

84. Sar. 3060, II-B-7, Room 72, level 5. Face from head of a hollow figurine; molded and beard attached to the chin; decoration on head may be tightly fitting cap or stylized hair; height, .05 m.; surface, pink (10YR 7/4).

85. Sar. 2388, II-C-8, level 2b. Head of figurine wearing wide headdress; pressed in a mold; traces of red paint remain on face over the red slip; height, .033 m.; surface, very pale brown (10YR 7.5/3).

86. Sar. 1362, II-B-7, level 4. Terracotta mask, with nostrils indicated on prominent nose; beard and moustache indicated with black paint; red paint or slip on face; height, .10 m.

87. Sar. 4229, II-C-2, level 4-2. Upper part of mask; height, .119 m.; surface, light red (2.5YR 6/6); eyebrows and hair have remains of black paint.

88. Sar. 4200, II-C-3, level 3-1. Lower part of terracotta mask with beard indicated by incised circles; surface highly burnished; height, .096 m.; surface, red (10R 4/6).

89. Sar. 3225, II-K-20, level 30-1. Ovoid hematite weight, flattened on the bottom; length, .026 m.; black.

90. Sar. 4204, II-Z-4, level 2-1. Cylinder seal of carnelian; length, .015 m.; light orange, translucent.

91. Sar. 3177, II-A-5, level 4-2. Miniature lamp bracket, with hole for attachment to peg, and small lamp in place within bracket; height, .084 m.; salmon-colored terracotta.

92. Sar. 2444, II-A-5, level 2d. Fragment of clay lamp with double spout; width of fragment, .12 m.; surface, salmon.

93. Sar. 4223, II-Z-4, level 2-2. Fragment of deep bowl, with inscription incised under the rim; length of fragment, .156 m.; surface, pink (5YR 7/4).

94. Sar. 2338, II-A/B-6, level 1. Base of vessel incised with inscription before firing; maximum measurement of preserved fragment, .07 m.; surface, salmon-red; trace of burnishing on preserved wall of the vessel.

95. Sar. 2214, II-C-9, level 2. Sherd with two-line inscription incised before firing; width, .082 m.; surface salmon.

96. Sar. 2429, II-A-7/8, level 3. Sherd inscribed before firing with nine letters below two horizontal grooves; width, .115 m.; surface, salmon color and burnished.

97. Sar. 2402, II-D-5, level 2d. Scaraboid stamp of green and brown stone, engraved with three-line inscription in mirror writing; pierced longitudinally for suspension; length, .019 m.

98. Sar. 4125, II-A-4, level 3. Ivory plaque with four lines of writing; .05 by .033 m.

99. Sar. 2265, II-B-5, level 2a. Glass disk bearing "Sign of Tanit" design; diameter, .01 m.; blue.

100. Sar. 3102, II-A-9, level 6. Fragment of jar handle impressed before firing with two lines of Ugaritic letters; handle is rectangular in section, except for five ridges on the upper side; the writing probably began near the point of juncture between the upper part of the handle and the body of the jar, and ran downward on the handle; length of upper curved surface of the preserved portion of handle, .10 m.; surface, buff; ware fairly coarse.

101. Sar. 3237, II-B-8, level 6. Storage jar; height, .50 m.; surface, very pale brown (10YR 8/3).

102. ———, II-B-8, level 7. Jar with spout at base; height, .265 m.; surface, very pale brown (10YR 8/3).

103. Sar. 3137, II-C-7, Room 10, level 22. Steatite mold

for casting jewelry, with funnels for liquid metal on sides; measurements, .056 by .059 m.; dark gray stone.

129-130. ———, II-A-4, level 3. Sandstone block carved with basin and channels; measurements, .28 by .32 by .20 m.

132. Sar. 3057, II-A-4, level 3. Faience figure of Bes, pierced through the headdress to serve as a pendant; height, .029 m.; surface, light blue.

133. Sar. 3200, II-A-4, level 3. Cat-headed human female figure standing against a plinth, which is pierced for suspension; height, .045 m.; light green faience.

134. Sar. 3007, II-A-4, level 3. Faience figure of Horus as a child; height, .052 m.; surface, light green.

135. Sar. 3013, II-A-4, level 3. Faience amulet of a sow attached to a base; height, .025 m.; surface, light green.

136. Sar. 3050, II-A-4, level 3. Wḏjet-amulet, pierced longitudinally; length, .059 m.; green faience, with green.

black on pupil and eyebrow; both sides have identical decoration.

137. right. Sar. 3005, II-A-4, level 3. Hollow terracotta figurine of woman holding stylized bird in her arms; height, .168 m.; surface, buff.

137. center. Sar. 3187, II-A-4, level 3. Fragment of terracotta sphinx throne; width, .127 m.; surface, pink (5YR 8/4); decoration of blue, red, and black paint.

137. left. Sar. 3188, II-A-4, level 3. Seated female figure playing a hand drum or tambourine; height, .185 m.; surface, salmon; decoration in red and black paint.

138. Sar. 4120, II-A-4, level 3. Head from sphinx throne (Fig. 137, center); height, .078 m.; surface, pink (5YR 8/4); decoration of blue and red paint.

139. Sar. 3030, II-A-4, level 3. Head of woman carved in ivory; height, .044 m.; back smoothed off.

140. Sar. 2293, II-A-4, level 2. Pottery figurine of seated pregnant woman; height, .145 m.; surface, buff; decoration in red paint.

Chronology of Preliminary Reports

The following preliminary reports and news accounts of the excavations have appeared:

1969: *New York Times*, Jan. 8, 1970.

1969, 1970: "The Roman Port at Sarafand (Sarepta): Preliminary Report on the Seasons of 1969 and 1970," *Bulletin du Musée de Beyrouth*, vol. 24, 1971, pp. 39-56.

1969, 1970, 1971, 1972: "Les fouilles de Sarepta," *Bible et Terre Sainte*, no. 157, Jan. 1974, pp. 4-14.

1970: *New York Times*, Aug. 22, 1970; "The Phoenician City of Sarepta," *Archaeology*, vol. 24, 1971, pp. 61-63.

1970, 1971: "The Phoenicians in their Homeland," *Expedition*, vol. 14, 1971, pp. 14-23.

1970, 1971, 1972: *Sarepta: A Preliminary Report on the Iron Age*, Museum Monograph, Philadelphia, 1975.

1971: *New York Times*, Sept. 2, 1971.

1972: *New York Times*, Aug. 21, 1972; "The 1972 Excavations at Sarepta (Lebanon)," *Rivista di studi fenici*, vol. 1, 1973, pp. 91-92.

1974: *Washington Post*, Nov. 15, 1974.

The Staff

William P. Anderson, 1970-74
Homer Athanassiou, 1972
Leila Badre, 1969-72, 1974
Patricia Cecil Bikai, 1969-72, 1974
Pierre Bikai, 1969-72, 1974
Julia Costello, 1972-73
Giocchino Falsone, 1971
Holly Hartquist, 1972-74
Ellen Herscher, 1972-73
Adrianna Hopper, 1971
John E. Huesman, 1969-72, 1974
Martha Joukowsky, 1969-73
Leila Khalidy, 1969-70
Issam Khalifeh, 1974
Marian Laaff, 1972
Susan Long, 1971, 1974
Thomas L. McClellan, 1969-72, 1974
Patrick McGovern, 1974
Magnus Ottosson, 1969-70, 1974
Pierre Proulx, 1970-72, 1974
William Stiebing, 1974
Sigurdur Orn Steingrimsson, 1971

Index

Library of Congress Cataloging in Publication Data

Pritchard, James Bennett, 1909-
    Recovering Sarepta, a Phoenician city.
    Includes index.
    1. Sarepta, Lebanon.   I. Title.
DS89.S37P74   939'.44   77-28304
ISBN 0-691-09378-4